Publishing as a Creative Industry

Book publishing is big business, contributing significant employment in the creative industries and adding billions to the global economy. Despite this, the sector is often overlooked in the creative industries' research tide. This book remedies this gap in knowledge, providing an examination of book publishing in the UK within the wider context of the creative industries and the existing academic discourse.

Balancing the tensions of art and commerce perhaps more than any other creative field, this book considers the position of the book publishing industry within the contemporary cultural economy. Through this focused analysis on the culture(s) and organisation(s) of book publishing in the UK, the author demonstrates how this creative industry reflects, and perpetuates, many of the key issues and challenges, including inequalities in representation, cultural and economic dominance of global conglomerates, and hierarchies of value, already recognised as central within the creative industries in the UK and beyond.

This concise book will be an essential read for academics, researchers, and students with an interest in the publishing industry and its position within the UK Creative Industries and cultural economy.

Stevie Marsden is Lecturer in the School of Arts and Creative Industries at Edinburgh Napier University, Edinburgh, Scotland, UK.

Routledge Research in the Creative and Cultural Industries

Series Editor: Ruth Rentschler

This series brings together book-length original research in cultural and creative industries from a range of perspectives. Charting developments in contemporary cultural and creative industries thinking around the world, the series aims to shape the research agenda to reflect the expanding significance of the creative sector in a globalised world.

Innovative Cultural Tourism in European Peripheries
Edited by Karol Jan Borowiecki, Antonella Fresa and José María Martín Civantos

Global Art Markets
History and Current Trends
Edited by Iain Robertson, Derrick Chong and Luís U. Afonso

The Political Economy of the Creative and Cultural Industries
Stitching Perspectives for Research, Policy and Practice
Leandro Valiati

Responsible Consumption and Production in the Creative and Cultural Industries
Actions, Policies, and Strategies for a Sustainable Future
Edited by Elisa Salvador and Ilaria Pappalepore

Publishing as a Creative Industry
Stevie Marsden

For more information about this series, please visit: www.routledge.com/Routledge-Research-in-the-Creative-and-Cultural-Industries/book-series/RRCCI

Publishing as a Creative Industry

Stevie Marsden

LONDON AND NEW YORK

First published 2025
by Routledge
4 Park Square, Milton Park, Abingdon, Oxon OX14 4RN

and by Routledge
605 Third Avenue, New York, NY 10158

Routledge is an imprint of the Taylor & Francis Group, an informa business

British Library Cataloguing-in-Publication Data
A catalogue record for this book is available from the British Library

ISBN: 978-1-032-03550-5 (hbk)
ISBN: 978-1-032-03552-9 (pbk)
ISBN: 978-1-003-18790-5 (ebk)

DOI: 10.4324/9781003187905

Typeset in Times New Roman
by Apex CoVantage, LLC

Contents

Acknowledgements

I would like to thank the editorial team at Routledge, Naomi and Terry, for their encouragement and patience throughout the process of writing this book. Thanks, also, to Dr Christina Neuwirth and Dr Claire Sedgwick for their advice and support. This one's for Parker.

Introduction

In April 2023, the Publishers Association reported that the UK's Publishing industry broke previous records in total sales, selling 669 million physical books in 2022 and earning £6.9 billion in revenue. This was up by 4% in 2021 (£6.7 billion) and up over 350% from ten years previously in 2012 (Flood, 2013). Despite the closure of brick and mortar bookshops during national lockdowns through 2020 to 2021 due to the coronavirus pandemic, UK publishing appeared to prove itself to be a hardy sector, selling more than 200 million print books in 2020 alone (Flood, 2021). When considered in relation to UK Creative Industries on the whole, publishing added 6.15% of the sector's overall contribution (£109 billion) to the UK economy in 2021 (Scott, 2022). This is more than the crafts sector, which contributes £3.4 billion (or 3.1% of the Creative Industries' overall contribution) per year (Crafts Council, 2014), and the music industry, which contributed £4 billion (3.7%) to the UK economy in 2021 (*UK Music urges Government to protect music industry*, 2022). Even at its pre-pandemic heights in 2018, the music industry contribution was £5.8 billion, which was slightly lower than that of Publishing, at £6.05 billion, in the same year (Page, 2019). The purpose of highlighting such figures is not to encourage economic point scoring or the hierarchising of art and culture in the UK but to emphasise the significant influence of publishing as a Creative Industries sector. Indeed, as will be discussed and scrutinised throughout this study, since the late twentieth century, the Creative Industries, both in the UK and elsewhere, have been discussed almost exclusively in terms of their economic contribution and (re)generation, particularly in policy discourse. This, as many commentators have identified and will be discussed in more detail presently, aligns with an apparent commitment to neoliberal economic, social, and cultural policy, which favours deregulation, privatisation, and the free market. As this study will evidence, publishing is a clear example of how Creative Industries function within such neoliberal capitalist frameworks.

However, despite its impressive economic contribution to the UK (cultural) economy and, therefore, its stake within the Creative Industries more broadly, publishing is an oft forgotten or overlooked member of the UK

DOI: 10.4324/9781003187905-1

government's Department for Digital, Culture, Media and Sport (DCMS) list of Creative Industries.[1] This is both in terms of its economic stability and provision, and its influence upon the UK cultural sector more broadly (the complexities of political interventions in, and categorisations of, the UK Creative Industries will be discussed in more detail later in this chapter). Not only can there be confusion surrounding what, exactly, publishing (as a Creative Industry) encompasses, but also it is a less visibly present member of the Creative Industries in the UK in terms of policy discourse and academic literature. The purpose of this book, therefore, is to re-examine the status of the UK's publishing industry as a Creative Industry and resituate (or reinstate) its position in relation to the UK's cultural and creative industries sector(s) more broadly. It will be argued that publishing not only shares many similarities and concurrences with other Creative Industries, but that it is also in a unique position of being one of the oldest industries that has both seen and had to respond to dramatic transformations in production and distribution practices, while maintaining traditional, and often problematic, business models and procedures. It is perhaps because of this long-standing history and stalwart status that publishing in the UK has been largely left to its own devices, becoming an economically lucrative private sector while maintaining an influential reputation as a key component of the UK's cultural identity and heritage. Yet, it is precisely because of these traits that an examination of the publishing sector and how it functions in relation to the broader socio-political and cultural dynamics of the UK Creative Industries is required. As Kate Oakley has argued:

> [T]here is some value, from the standpoint of what we used to call industrial policy (and now more prosaically refer to as business support), in delineating the group of industries concerned with cultural production and analysing their needs, identities and responses to interventions.
>
> (Oakley, 2004, p. 72)

Accordingly, this study aims to fill the current gap in cultural studies and creative industries discourse to characterise publishing's specific role as a Creative Industry.

Why Book Publishing?

Before moving into further discussion of the publishing industry in the UK, it is important to clarify some definitions and explore the extensive existing literature pertaining to the Creative Industries in the UK. As of writing, the UK Creative Industries, as defined by DCMS, include the following sectors:

- Advertising and marketing
- Architecture

- Crafts
- Product design, graphic design and fashion design
- Film, TV, video, radio and photography
- IT, software, video games and computer services
- Publishing and translation
- Museums, galleries and libraries
- Music, performing arts, visual arts and cultural education

(*Creative industries economic estimates*, 2017)

The DCMS evolved from the Department of National Heritage (DNH) which was founded in 1992 by the then Conservative Prime Minister John Major. The DNH was created 'to amalgamate a number of functions related to the arts, broadcasting, film, sport, architecture and historic sites, royal parks and tourism' (*Department of National Heritage*, 1993), but on a change of government in 1997, the DNH became the DCMS. Between July 2017 and February 2023, the department was renamed the Department for Digital, Culture, Media and Sport, expanding the remit of the division to include 'building a shared society and digital connectivity' (*A Short Guide to the Department for Digital, Culture, Media and Sport—National Audit Office (NAO) overview*, 2017, p. 5). It seems that the purpose of this expansion of the remit of the department was to focus on the advancement of the telecommunications and digital infrastructure of the UK, as well as increasing powers to regulate 'Big Tech' and online spaces (Johnstone, 2017). However, on the announcement of the reversion to the Department of Culture, Media and Sport in February 2023, the UK government claimed that a 're-focused Department for Culture, Media and Sport will recognise the importance of these industries to our economy and build on the UK's position as a global leader in the creative arts' (*PM: Making government deliver for the British people*, 2023).

When it comes to the specific definitions of sectors included within the DCMS, several, including publishing, are vague or broad in scope. Crafts, performing arts, visual arts, and cultural education, for example, can encompass many different forms of cultural production and also overlap with other categories within the DCMS list. Equally, identifying exactly what Publishing should and does include can be tricky. In the results of a 2020 Business Impacts of Coronavirus Survey (BICS), DCMS categorised Publishing as including 'Newspapers, academic Publishing, books, magazines etc.' (*DCMS BICS round 2*, 2020). However, this conflation of the vastly different publishing industries in the UK is unhelpful. Newspaper and magazine publishing in the UK functions, and is regulated, in a way very different to book publishing. From financial and business models to the acquiring and commissioning of content, books, magazines, and newspapers currently function in fundamentally dissimilar ways. For example, taking books from submission and acceptance to publication can take anywhere from several months to a number of years. Newspapers and magazines, on the other hand, run on a much faster production timeframe, with newspapers in particular running on hours and days, as opposed to weeks or months at a time. This also impacts the funding models of the industries, with newspapers and magazines relying more heavily on advertising and subscriptions (and both industries have struggled to maintain traditional areas of revenue due to the abundance of free information online, see e.g. Majid, 2022; and Reuters, 2022). Book publishers, on the other hand, tend to require an initial outlay of investment that will (in theory) be earned back once a book is published. Profits are also then used to fund other publications, and it is this model that makes book publishing one of the riskiest, and consequently risk-averse, Creative Industries.

Further, newspapers and magazines are monitored and regulated in ways that book publishing is not. The Independent Press Standards Organisation (IPSO) is the independent regulator for newspaper and magazine publishing in the UK. According to its website, IPSO 'hold[s] newspapers and magazines to account for their actions, protect individual rights, uphold high standards of journalism and help to maintain freedom of expression for the press' (IPSO, no date). There is no equivalent regulatory body for book publishing in the UK. There are organisations like the Publishers Association, the industry's trade organisation (membership fees for which are calculated according to a publishing company's annual turnover), and the Society of Authors, a trade union for 'all types of writers, illustrators and literary translators' that provides support, advice, and advocacy for creatives in publishing (The Society of Authors, no date). But while these groups may conduct research into and comment on the state of the industry and problematic or unfair practices, they do not investigate publishers or facilitate corrections and apologies based on agreed-upon industry standards like those which are established for magazines and newspapers.

Such divergences in the operations of these different publishing industries make them difficult for this study to consider them, at least conceptually, as one distinct industry. This book, therefore, is taking a narrower and more specific view of the publishing industry in the UK, focusing specifically on book publishing which, as will be discussed in more detail in Chapter 1, includes key sectors such as trade/consumer publishing, academic publishing, and educational publishing. The narrower focus on book publishing is deliberate and necessary for both practical and scholarly reasons. It would be practically very difficult to address the entire gamut of publishing output in the UK within this slim volume. Newspaper and magazine publishing in the UK each require, and deserve, their own dedicated analyses of their position within the UK Creative Industries. Additionally, given that the publishing of books, magazines, and newspapers works in such incomparably different ways, it would not be prudent to attempt to discuss the machinations of these different types of publishing as if they are analogous, and while the purpose of this book is to draw attention to the elements of book publishing that are aligned with, and reflect, aspects of other Creative Industries, a distinct focus is still necessary to provide clear insight and argument.

Relatedly, the scope of this study is purposeful in its attention on the UK Creative Industries and economic market. While there will be reference to other markets when relevant, this study considers book publishing within the specific framework of the sociopolitical and cultural discourse surrounding the Creative Industries in the UK. It will be argued that book publishing navigates a multidimensional role within the Creative Industries in the UK, which is complicated by hierarchies of value and romanticised views of how the industry works and its purpose, thus bringing to the fore the juxtaposition of cultural value(s) and commerciality. Such issues have been identified in other Creative Industries, but the existing literature has typically considered publishing as an addendum to more detailed studies of other Creative Industries (or has not considered it at all), rather than as a focus of study within the context of Creative Industry discourse in and of itself.

Defining the Creative Industries

To establish the broader context within which book publishing functions as a Creative Industry, it is important to provide an overview of the existing literature concerning the Creative Industries and their status in relation to UK society, culture, and politics. There is an extensive body of academic work dedicated to understanding the Creative Industries in the UK which provides an apt foundation from which to build an understanding of publishing as a Creative Industry. There has been much in the way of scholarship debating the values and preferences of terminologies when it comes to cultural/creative industries' policy and discourse, and it is not necessary to rehash these arguments here. However, given that this study favours the term Creative Industries specifically, it is worthwhile spending some time explaining why this is the case.

Galloway and Dunlop have argued that the 'terminology currently used in creative industries policy lacks rigour and is frequently inconsistent and confusing' (2007, p. 17). They trace this back to the confused interchangeability of the use of 'cultural industries' and 'creative industries', which Galloway and Dunlop consider to be a shortcoming in the clear conceptualisation of each distinct term.

Smith and McKinlay echo this, arguing that the issue with the idea of the 'cultural industries' is that the 'concept of culture is notoriously opaque, embracing as it does the role of tradition, identity, values and social belonging' (Smith and McKinlay, 2009, p. 4). Smith and McKinlay continue, noting how Cultural Industries 'also lacks a strong connection to a political economy, as commercialisation of life styles and youth cultures are within industries (fashion and clothing) with conventional mass or batch production labour processes, and are not usefully defined as creative' (Smith and

McKinlay, 2009, p. 4). This distinction is significant to consider in relation to book publishing as, although it often deals with inherently creative materials, the purpose of which may be the creation of literature or art for its own sake, at its core, book publishing is an industry of mass production of commercial products that need to be sold and bought, usually at large quantities, to remain economically viable. If it is to be narrowed further still, book publishing has established itself as an industry that specialises in a unique product—the book—the basic form of which typically remains unchanged. Paring our understanding of the industry down to this level is important, because it reminds us of the industrialised mass production of the product, a fact which is often overlooked, or veiled, by both the industry and its commentators because of an idealised perception of the cultural value(s) of literature and the written word. The contemporary publishing industry arguably intertwines the 'types' of cultural industries that Theodor Adorno identified. As Garnham explains, Adorno makes a

> distinction between those cultural industries which employ industrial technology to produce or reproduce cultural goods which are themselves produced largely by craft means (for example, books, records), and those where the cultural form is itself industrial (newspapers, television, film).
> (1990, p. 157)

While there are book publishers, printers, and binders who will use 'industrial technology' but take a more artisanal or 'craft' approach to the publishing production process, such as the Folio Society, an employee-owned publisher which specialises in 'crafting exquisite, illustrated editions' of books that have often limited runs and have higher price points (non-limited illustrated hardback editions of Anthony Burgess' *A Clockwork Orange* and Irvine Welsh's *Trainspotting* cost £44.95 and £60, respectively (The Folio Society, no date)), on the whole, the contemporary book publishing industry is arguably managed on an industrial scale akin to newspapers, television, and film. This is demonstrated by the fact that many of the largest publishers are now owned not only by global media corporations but also intertwined with industrial processes of production (particularly printing and distribution but also the commercial and marketing industry complexes of publishing) and the kinds of cultural and economic statuses embedded within publishing. Advances for authors (celebrity or otherwise) can run into millions (Barack and Michelle Obama signed a joint book deal in 2017 worth $65 million (£52.5 million) (Campbell, 2017)), and bestselling books can equally earn tens of millions: since publication in 2019, the graphic novel-cum-self-help book *The Boy, the Mole, the Fox and the Horse* by Charlie Mackesy has 'sold 1.62 million copies for £18.1m in the UK' (Brown, 2023). Accordingly, contemporary book publishing blends Adorno's distinctions between cultural industries that utilise 'industrial technology' to reproduce 'crafted' cultural goods and industries 'where the cultural form is itself industrial' (Garnham, 1990, p. 157). However, this book argues that there has been a reluctance to consider book publishing in such terms because the rhetoric surrounding the industry is one which focuses on the inherent virtuousness of the act of sharing the written word and deplores notions of it functioning as a commercial enterprise focused on selling a product. The problem with this perspective is the fact that it contributes to the exploitation of the labour required for the industry to continue. The perpetuation of romanticised idea(l)s of the significance of the cultural and social value of working in publishing, or being published, contributes to the surplus of supply (of content to be published or people seeking employment) for the actual demand (or opportunities and access) within the industry.

To return to the Cultural versus Creative Industries debate, Smith and McKinlay argue that, '*Creative industries* is the new dominant and politically fashionable term being more inclusive of new and old sectors, such as theatre and new media, but sufficiently discriminating so as to produce a relatively clear industry category' (emphasis in original, Smith and McKinlay, 2009, p. 4). Despite arguments that 'creative' is also broad and fails to 'discriminate between scientific/technical creativity and artistic creativity' (see also Hesmondhalgh who also argues that 'Creativity' is a 'looser word than culture', 2008, p. 560), Smith and McKinlay favour Creative Industries as a term in their work to encapsulate the shared features of 'innovation, risk, uncertainty, performativity and differentiation from repeat or mass production sectors' (Smith and McKinlay, 2009, p. 4). While Smith and McKinlay hint at the political influences of the favouring of Creative Industries, others have been more forthright in their alignment of the political impetus that swayed the preference for using Creative Industries over Cultural Industries. Galloway and Dunlop argue that 'for most commentators it was with the election of "New Labour" in Britain in 1997 that the decisive shift in terminology occurred, and the term "creative industries" reached an ascendence in public policy' (Galloway and Dunlop, 2007, p. 18). Pratt has argued that the move towards Creative, over Cultural, Industries was a deliberate move on the part of the New Labour government who positioned themselves as politically centrist and wished to distance themselves from 'cultural industries policies [that] were tainted with left-leaning "old" Labour values' (Pratt, 2005, p. 32). Hesmondhalgh has not only reiterated this but also noted that the terminology had been used by other governments:

> *Creative industries* is a concept that has since been widely adopted in the spheres of cultural policy and higher education. Its first major policy use appears to have been by the British Labour government elected in

> 1997, though there were important precedents in other countries, notably the Australian Labor government's *Creative Nation* initiative of 1994.
>
> (2008, p. 559)

Other countries, such as France, Canada, and New Zealand, were also invested in instituting creative industries policies during the late 1980s into the early 2000s (Hesmondhalgh and Pratt, 2005; Volkerling, 2001).

Pratt offers a compelling argument for the use of the term Cultural Industries, suggesting that due to the Creative Industries' link to the political programme of the New Labour government in the UK, it is a term of 'little analytical value' and that 'at least the cultural industries have a putative activity (such as film-making or writing a book) to produce a "cultural" object' whereas 'the creative industries' object is creativity itself' (Pratt, 2005, p. 33). However, the fact that creative and cultural production has played an important role in the UK's neoliberal socio-political and economic landscape in recent years is a key context for this study on book publishing in the UK, and given that 'Creative Industries' was the preferred term in the political parlance of turn of the century Britain, this is the term that is favoured throughout this study.

Things Can Only Get Better

A 1997 'landslide' general election victory for the UK's (New) Labour party brought in a new era of British politics following nearly two decades of Conversative party rule, led predominantly by Prime Minister Margaret Thatcher, whose political ideology favoured capitalism and free markets, privatisation, minimalistic government (so-called small state or low regulatory interference), and a suppression of trade union and labour rights. Despite seemingly being on separate ends of the political spectrum, New Labour sustained some of the previous governments' neoliberal tendencies, particularly in terms of the UK's Creative Industries.[2] Writing in 2004, Oakley argued that New Labour 'put its commitment to the creative industries very much at the heart of its initial message', but that after five years in government, 'a number of severe problems [were] becoming apparent in [New Labour's] approach' (Oakley, 2004, p. 68). While Oakley acknowledged that some of these issues were legacies of underinvestment, she also argued that others 'result[ed] directly from the current approach' (Oakley, 2004, p. 68). Oakley is not the only scholar to discuss the rise of the contemporary Creative Industries in Britain in terms of the sociopolitical and economic climate of the time, but before moving into a discussion of how New Labour and neoliberal political ideology have influenced the creative industries, and book publishing specifically, it is worth taking a moment to explain how neoliberalism is being understood herewith.

Steger and Roy explain that neoliberalism is an 'economistic ideology, which . . . puts the production and exchange of material goods at the heart of the human experience' (Steger and Roy, 2010, p. 12) and argue that the first wave of neoliberalism came in the 1980s with the rise of Reaganomics (in the US) and Thatcherism (in the UK). As Carlquist and Phelps note, neoliberalism is 'associated with the favoring of free market competition and private property rights, reduction or abolishment of government intervention and expenditure, and valuation of individual "freedom of choice"' (Carlquist and Phelps, 2014, p. 1231). Carlquist and Phelps continue, highlighting the fundamentally problematic nature of neoliberal ideology:

> Although often represented in everyday discourse . . . as an 'efficient' and self-evident way of social organization, neoliberalism is associated with a disproportionate accrual of wealth and opportunity among certain groups. In particular, critics point out that neoliberalism benefits multinational corporations and the financial sector, as well as particular government agencies and international organizations. When put into practice, neoliberal policy has produced increasing social and economic inequalities within countries as well as between countries and regions.
>
> (Carlquist and Phelps, 2014, p. 1231)

Steger and Roy echo this, arguing that there are key agents, or 'codifiers', of the 'three dimensions of neoliberalism': ideology, a mode of governance, and policy package(s) (Steger and Roy, 2010, p. 11). According to Steger and Roy, such codifiers are:

> [G]lobal elites that include managers and executives of large transnational corporations, corporate lobbyists, influential journalists and public-relations specialists, intellectuals writing for a large public audiences, celebrities and top entertainers, state bureaucrats, and politicians.
>
> (Steger and Roy, 2010, p. 11)

Both Carlquist and Phelps', and Steger and Roy's, framing of neoliberalism and its mechanisms are particularly helpful for this study of book publishing. It is posited in this analysis that not only are some of the key 'codifiers' of neoliberalism also central agents in book publishing, notably transnational corporations, journalists, 'intellectuals', celebrities, and top entertainers (both in terms of celebrity authors and authors who become celebrities) but also that book publishing in the UK runs on an inherently neoliberal model of business which predominantly benefits global conglomerates and has contributed to 'increasing social and economic inequalities' (Carlquist and Phelps, 2014, p. 1231).

What is more, as Oakley has argued using the work of Bevir (2005), there were specific elements to New Labour's form of neoliberalism that meant it aligned, and continues to align, even more comfortably with publishing. Oakley contends:

> [T]he particular development of neoliberalism represented by New Labour is better captured in Bevir's argument (2005) about the importance of institutionalist ideas for New Labour. [Bevir] sees these as a distinct form of neoliberalism, in the emphasis on networks characterised by social and ethical norms, as opposed to a focus purely on marketisation.
>
> (Oakley, 2011, p. 281)

Publishing, like other Creative Industries, relies on social networks for, as Eikhof and Warhurst put it, 'getting in and getting on' (Eikhof and Warhurst, 2013, p. 502); accordingly, despite its traditional focus on increased competition and individualism, the importance of social associations and connections to build one's own status and credibility was central to post-New Labour Creative Industry neoliberalism. But, also, publishing is a Creative Industry that operates on a duality of idealistic notions of creative enterprise and free-market capitalism. While not mutually exclusive, there is a particular discordance in the culture and rhetoric of publishing that favours and perpetuates a (often rose-tinted) perspective of creative work and production that is disassociated from the essence (and inherent inequities) of private business and commercialisation. As Robert Hewison notes when discussing the emergence of New Labour and such sociocultural and existential animosities:

> Creative Britain would be populated by young and eager people, who, in spite of their techno-savvy, clung to the romantic image of the struggling artist, whose individualism would make the breakthrough that justified their insecurities and self-exploitation. Without the creatives, production and consumption would grind to a halt.
>
> (Hewison, 2014, pp. 5–6)

Sarah Brouillette has also discussed this 'romanticisation' of the creative worker in her formative study on literature and writing through the lens of post-Thatcher neoliberalism and New Labour's Creative Industries, *Literature and the Creative Economy*. Brouillette problematises the notion of creative work and the creative worker—specifically writing and writers, in her case—pushing back against what she calls the fundamental contradictions of 'creative-economy rhetoric' which posits that creative work is 'at once newly valuable to capitalism and romantically honorable and free' (Brouillette, 2014, p. 4). Brouillette's work is currently the closest we have to a discussion of book publishing as a creative industry that has embedded neoliberal principles of creative work and production, but her focus remains on the writer as creative worker, whereas this examination of the industry takes several steps back in the book production process to look at the publishing industrial (and cultural) complexes that fortify and sustain models of exploitation within creative work in publishing.

All of this said, this study recognises that neoliberalism is a term and concept that has been problematised. Flew has argued that there is 'conceptual elasticity' to the term and that 'the evidence of whether we are in an era of neo-liberalism remains decidedly mixed, not least because there seems to be little agreement on what evidence of it would be' (Flew, 2011, p. 190). Indeed, Flew goes as far to suggest that:

> In light of these problems with the concept of neo-liberalism, I think it is reasonable to say that, whatever other issues or problems arise with the concept of creative industries as either analytical concept or policy discourse, the criticism that it is emblematic of or furthers neo-liberalism is one that now needs to be discounted.
>
> (Flew, 2011, p. 191)

Flew's discounting of neoliberalism granted, it is still considered a useful framework for this study since, because it has been so frequently applied to critical analyses of the creative and/or cultural industries, it would feel like a conceptual omission to not consider it a viable framework by which to examine the contemporary publishing industry. Accordingly, while acknowledging the flawed nature of the term, this study finds Newsinger's argument that 'neoliberalism is best understood as a project of upward capital redistribution as opposed to a fundamentalist theoretical conviction in the natural ubiquity and efficacy of unfettered markets' helpful in explaining the inherent tensions and dichotomies of the term (Newsinger, 2015, p. 311).

Book Structure

This book is split into three key chapters which explore the issues discussed herewith in relation to the UK book publishing industry. Chapter 1, 'The Publishing Market Today', provides a detailed overview of the publishing industry as it currently functions. The chapter offers a summary of the key market sectors within the industry—consumer/trade publishing, academic publishing, and educational publishing—and discusses how each sector has developed through decades of conglomeration to favour monolithic publishers and/or massive media corporations who view publishing as one arm of a diverse portfolio of information and knowledge dissemination. Chapter 2, 'Searching for "Diversity" in Publishing (and the Creative Industries)', examines the current debates regarding workforce 'diversity' within the UK Publishing industry, demonstrating how Publishing replicates the well-documented inequities in representation among the creative industries workforce, particularly in relation to gender, race and ethnicity, disability, and class. Further, the chapter problematises the terminology of 'diversity' and how it has been used in creative industry policy discourse as a catch-all term to refer to anyone who is not white, middle-class, cis-gendered (and typically male), heterosexual, and non-disabled. Indeed, Chapter 2 demonstrates how publishing, as one of the oldest Creative Industries in the UK, is not only one of the worst Creative Industries in terms of workforce representation in several areas but has also been one of the slowest industries to reflect on its own systemic inequalities. Chapter 3, 'Publishing Hierarchies: Culture, Commerce, and Capitalism', argues that while publishing does share many similarities with other Creative Industries in terms of workforce composition and neoliberal values, book publishing is a unique sector in terms of how the cultural allure and ascendency of books dominate the perceptions of the industry and how it works. Such perceptions of publishing as being an inherently noble and rewarding endeavour have enabled the industry to be one which exploits its content creators (writers) and producers (the workforce behind production processes). As a result, the rhetoric surrounding work and progress within the industry, which is often framed in overly romanticised terms like love and passion, perpetuates the neoliberal ideals underpinning the industry (and the Creative Industries more widely). Finally, this study ends with a Conclusion, providing a summary of key arguments and propositions for further research and thought.

As previously noted, the purpose of this book is to examine the specific conditions and attributes of the UK book publishing industry. It has evolved from the author's view that, despite publishing being demonstrative of some of the key issues and concerns raised by existing scholarship and discourse pertaining to the Creative Industries, there is little scholarly work exploring publishing within this context. Therefore, this book hopes to provide insight into how UK Book Publishing operates as a Creative Industry and start a conversation about its status as an area of study in relation to other creative industries and related scholarship.

Notes

1 For example in *Creative Labour: Working in the Creative Industries*, Smith and McKinlay identify the creative industries as 'film, theatre, television, radio, arts and new media' (Smith and McKinlay, 2009).

2 The connections between the Conservative and New Labour governments did not go unnoticed: when asked what her greatest achievement as Prime Minister was, Thatcher reportedly responded 'Tony Blair and New Labour' (Low, 2023).

References

Bevir , M. (2005) *New Labour: A critique*. London: Routledge.

Brouillette, S. (2014) *Literature and the Creative Economy*. Stanford: Stanford University Press.

Brown, L. (2023) 'Mackesy's the boy, the mole, the fox and the horse sells into 50 languages', *The Bookseller*. Available at: https://www.thebookseller.com/news/mackesys-the-boy-the-mole-the-fox-and-the-horse-sells-into-50-languages (Accessed: 6 August 2023).

Campbell, L. (2017) 'PRH scoops book deal with Obamas', *The Bookseller*. Availableat:https://www.thebookseller.com/news/prh-scoops-obamas-book-deal-499511 (Accessed: 6 August 2023).

Carlquist, E. and Phelps, J. (2014) 'Neoliberalism', In T. Teo (ed.) *Encyclopedia of Critical Psychology*. New York: Springer New York, pp. 1231–1237. Available at: https://doi.org/10.1007/978-1-4614-5583-7_390.

Crafts Council. (2014) *Measuring the Craft Economy: Defining and Measuring Craft: Report 3*.

Creative Industries Economic Estimates. (2017) *GOV.UK*. Available at: https://www.gov.uk/government/collections/creative-industries-economic-estimates (Accessed: 16 May 2023).

DCMS. (2020) *BICS Round 2, Media and Creative Industries Subsectors—GOV.UK*. Available at: https://assets.publishing.service.gov.uk/government/uploads/system/uploads/attachment_data/file/943200/DCMS_BICS_Round_2_Data_tables_MediaAndCreativeIndustries.csv/preview(Accessed: 16 May 2023).

Department of National Heritage. (1993) *GOV.UK*. Available at: https://www.gov.uk/government/organisations/department-of-national-heritage (Accessed: 16 May 2023).

Eikhof, D.R. and Warhurst, C. (2013) 'The promised land? Why social inequalities are systemic in the creative industries', *Employee Relations*, 35(5), pp. 495–508. Available at: http://doi.org.napier.idm.oclc.org/10.1108/ER-08-2012-0061.

Flew, T. (2011) *The Creative Industries: Culture and Policy*. London, United Kingdom: SAGE Publications, Limited. Available at: http://ebookcentral.proquest.com/lib/napier/detail.action?docID=820089 (Accessed: 25 October 2024).

Flood, A. (2013) 'Printed book sales' decline slowed in 2012', *The Guardian*, 9 January. Available at: https://www.theguardian.com/books/2013/jan/09/printed-book-sales-2012 (Accessed: 16 May 2023).

Flood, A. (2021) 'Book sales defy pandemic to hit eight-year high', *The Guardian*, 25 January. Available at: https://www.theguardian.com/books/2021/jan/25/bookshops-defy-pandemic-to-record-highest-sales-for-eight-years (Accessed: 16 May 2023).

The Folio Society. (no date) *Illustrated Hardcover Fiction Books: Novels*, The Folio Society. Available at: https://www.foliosociety.com/uk/fiction (Accessed: 27 October 2024).

Galloway, S. and Dunlop, S. (2007) 'A critique of definitions of the cultural and creative industries in public policy', *International Journal of Cultural Policy*, 13(1), pp. 17–31. Available at: https://doi.org/10.1080/10286630701201657.

Garnham, N. (1990) *Capitalism and Communication: Global Culture and the Economics of Information*. SAGE.

Hesmondhalgh, D. (2008) 'Cultural and creative industries', in T. Bennett and J. Frow (eds.) *The SAGE Handbook of Cultural Analysis*. SAGE, pp. 552–569.

Hesmondhalgh, D. and Pratt, A.C. (2005) 'Cultural industries and cultural policy', *International Journal of Cultural Policy*, 11(1), pp. 1–13. Available at: https://doi.org/10.1080/10286630500067598.

Hewison, R. (2014) *Cultural Capital: The Rise and Fall of Creative Britain*. London: Verso.

IPSO (no date) *What We Do*. Available at: https://www.ipso.co.uk/what-we-do/ (Accessed: 16 May 2023).

Johnstone, R. (2017) *DCMS Gets New Name in Digital Rebrand*. Available at: https://www.civilserviceworld.com/news/article/dcms-gets-new-name-in-digital-rebrand (Accessed: 16 May 2023).

Low, V. (2023) 'I admire your resolve, Margaret Thatcher told Tony Blair', 6 August. Available at: https://www.thetimes.co.uk/article/i-admire-your-resolve-margaret-thatcher-told-tony-blair-288tjxfst (Accessed: 6 August 2023).

Majid, A. (2022) 'Charted: How has the UK consumer magazine industry evolved? Two decades of change', *Press Gazette*, 25 August. Available at: https://pressgazette.co.uk/publishers/magazines/uk-consumer-magazine-industry-charts/ (Accessed: 17 May 2023).

National Audit Office (NAO). (2017) *A Short Guide to the Department for Digital, Culture, Media and Sport—National Audit Office (NAO) Overview*. Availableat:https://www.nao.org.uk/overviews/a-short-guide-to-the-department-for-digital-culture-media-and-sport/ (Accessed: 16 May 2023).

Newsinger, J. (2015) 'A cultural shock doctrine? Austerity, the neoliberal state and the creative industries discourse', *Media, Culture & Society*, 37(2), pp. 302–313. Available at: https://doi.org/10.1177/0163443714560134.

Oakley, K. (2004) 'Not so cool Britannia: The role of the creative industries in economic development', *International Journal of Cultural Studies*, 7(1), pp. 67–77. Available at: https://doi.org/10.1177/1367877904040606.

Oakley, K. (2011) 'In its own image: New Labour and the cultural workforce', *Cultural Trends*, 20(3–4), pp. 281–289.

Page, B. (2019) 'Total UK publishing revenues down 2% in 2018; consumer book market stable', *The Bookseller*. Available at: https://www.thebookseller.com/news/uks-2018-revenues-down-2-amid-major-digital-swing-academic-publishers-1027311 (Accessed: 16 May 2023).

PM: Making Government Deliver for the British People. (2023) *GOV.UK*. Available at: https://www.gov.uk/government/news/making-government-deliver-for-the-british-people (Accessed: 16 May 2023).

Pratt, A.C. (2005) 'Cultural industries and public policy: An oxymoron?', *International Journal of Cultural Policy*, 11(1), pp. 31–44. Available at: https://doi.org/10.1080/10286630500067739.

Reuters. (2022) 'UK newspapers at risk as investors shun the sector, report finds', *Reuters*, 6 May. Available at: https://www.reuters.com/world/uk/uk-media-industry-facing-low-profitability-says-government-report-2022-05-06/ (Accessed: 17 May 2023).

Scott, E. (2022) 'Arts and creative industries: The case for a strategy'. Available at: https://lordslibrary.parliament.uk/arts-and-creative-industries-the-case-for-a-strategy/ (Accessed: 16 May 2023).

Smith, C. and McKinlay, A. (eds.). (2009) *Creative Labour: Working in the Creative Industries*. Hampshire: Palgrave Macmillan.

The Society of Authors. (no date) *About | The Society of Authors*. Available at: https://societyofauthors.org/about-us (Accessed: 17 May 2023).

Steger, M.B. and Roy, R.K. (2010) *Neoliberalism: A Very Short Introduction*. New York: Oxford University Press.

UK Music Urges Government to Protect Music Industry. (2022). Available at: https://www.prsformusic.com/press/2022/uk-music-urges-government-to-protect-music-industry (Accessed: 16 May 2023).

Volkerling, M. (2001) 'From cool Britannia to hot nation: "Creative industries" policies in Europe, Canada and New Zealand', *International Journal of Cultural Policy*, 7(11), pp. 437–455. Available at: https://doi.org/10.1080/10286630109358155.

1 The Publishing Market Today

As noted earlier, the UK's publishing industry contributed £6.9 billion to the UK economy in revenue in 2022 (Publishers Association, 2023). How this is divided by print and digital publishing sales, and the home and export market, is illustrated in Figure 1.1. Between 2020 and 2022, the publishing industry (like many others) suffered due to national lockdowns in response to the global COVID-19 pandemic. Nielsen BookScan, the UK's data provider for book sales, reported that 2020 and 2021 were missing 17 and 10 weeks of sales data, respectively. The year 2022, therefore, was the first year of an apparent return to 'normality' for the industry, and the industry appeared to thrive.[1]

This data can be broken down further into distinct sectors which make up book publishing in the UK, namely consumer (or trade), academic, and educational Publishing (these will be discussed in turn below). This is not to suggest that these categorisations are the only way to examine a cross-section of contemporary book publishing in the UK, but such categorisation of the industry's financial (and cultural) contribution to the UK Creative Industries (in accordance with the Publishers Association's 'A Year in Publishing' report 2023) provides a concise means by which to examine the market today.

Consumer/Trade Publishing

Consumer publishing (or trade publishing) is, according to Clark and Phillips, 'the most visible part of the industry' (Clark and Phillips, 2020, p. 93).[2] The titles of consumer publishers are:

> Displayed prominently in high street bookshops and other outlets, receive considerable mass-media coverage and are aimed mainly at the indefinable 'general reader', and sometimes at the enthusiast or specialist reader. They form the mainstay of public libraries, and in some cases penetrate academic markets. . . . Consumer book publishing is the high-risk end of the business: book failures are frequent but the rewards from 'bestsellers'—some of which are quite unexpected—can be great. The potential readers

DOI: 10.4324/9781003187905-2

> are varied, spread thinly through the population, expensive to reach, difficult to identify, and have tastes and interests that can be described generally but are not easily matched to a particular book. Publisher bet to a great extent on their judgment of public taste and interests—notoriously unpredictable.
>
> (Clark and Phillips, 2020, p. 93)

Consumer publishing, therefore, is often considered to be understood as 'mainstream' book publishing, accounting for the kinds of books that will become bestsellers and make household names out of authors, such as Stephen King, Hilary Mantel, and J.K. Rowling. It includes genre fiction (e.g. horror, sci-fi, romance) as well as literary fiction, poetry, and non-fiction (cookbooks, memoirs, history, popular science, travel, etc.), and caters for the children's, young adult, and adult markets.

Figure 1.2 provides a more detailed view of the amount, in GBP, that the consumer publishing sector contributed to the UK publishing industry's overall £6.9 billion income in 2022. As demonstrated, the consumer market was up on the basis of previous years' figures (as may be expected, given the lingering issues from the pandemic in 2021), with particularly significant increases in the export market for both print (15%) and digital (8%). The minor downturn in non-fiction was noted by some, being described as a 'plateau' by the Chief Executive Officer of literary agency, Curtis Brown, Jonny Geller (The Bookseller Editorial Team, 2023). Significantly, while Tim Whiting, managing director of Bonnier Books UK's Black & White Publishing division, suggested that the 'retail environment was tough generally', due to the UK cost-of-living crisis and economic uncertainties (which would arguably affect all sectors in consumer publishing), Geller argued that the issue with non-fiction specifically

UK Publishing Market Income 2022		
	£	% increase or decrease in the previous year
Print	3,800,000,000	↑3
Digital	3,100,000,000	↑5
Home market	2,700,000,000	↓1
Export market	4,100,000,000	↑8
Total	6,900,000,000	↑4

Figure 1.1 UK Publishing Market Income 2022 (adapted from Publishers Association, 2023)

UK Consumer Market 2022		
	£	% increase or decrease in the previous year
Print (home market)	1,200,000,000	↑2
Digital (home market)	261,000,000	↑2
Print (export market)	662,000,000	↑15
Digital (export market)	162,000,000	↑8
Total income	2,300,000,000	↑2
By sector:		
Fiction	797,000,000	↑9
Audio	164,000,000	↑8
Non-fiction	1,000,000,000	↓2
Children's	429,000,000	↑1

Figure 1.2 UK Consumer Publishing Market Income 2022 (adapted from Publishers Association, 2023)

was that it was 'compet[ing] with the best Netflix documentaries and needs specialists or unique voices to prove to readers it is worth spending so much time with a book' (The Bookseller Editorial Team, 2023).

Consumer publishing is dominated by the 'Big Five' publishers: Penguin Random House, Pan Macmillan, Hachette, HarperCollins, and Simon & Schuster. This was previously the 'Big Six', but the merging of Penguin and Random House to become Penguin Random House (or PRH) in 2013 brought two of the largest book publishers in the world together. The merger would see the publisher have 'over 10,000 employees worldwide and publish more than 15,000 new titles every year across 250 imprints', and it was estimated that the 'new trade publishing powerhouse' would have an annual revenue of $3.9 billion (*Publisher's Weekly*, 2013). This so-called 'mega-merger' did not go unchallenged, with many in the industry sharing concerns about the loss of a publisher through consolidation and the monopolistic threat that such a dominating company may pose. Despite calls from the Authors Guild in the US for the Department of Justice (DOJ) to provide 'close scrutiny [of the merger] from anti-trust officials' (Carter, 2012), the DOJ approved the merger 'without conditions', indicating that there was no concern about the threat of market dominance (Cader, 2013). However, an attempt by PRH to acquire fellow 'Big Five' publisher Simon & Schuster (S&S) for over $2 billion in 2020 ultimately fell through following the filing of a complaint by the DOJ in November 2021, which stated that the acquisition would lead to an 'elimination of head-to-head competition' between PRH and S&S and also potentially harm 'best-selling authors by lessening incentives to give competitive pre-publication advances' (Blackwell, 2022). Bertelsmann, the German media group who own Penguin Random House, were prepared to appeal the decision but were unable to 'convince Paramount Global, Simon & Schuster's owner, to extend their deal agreement and appeal the judge's decision' (*The Guardian*, 2022).

Such cases demonstrate not only the monolithic status of some of the largest publishers in the world but also how such companies now belong within a much larger mass-media economy. Indeed, all of the Big Five publishers are part of major multinational media companies. Penguin Random House was purchased by the German multinational media conglomerate, Bertelsmann, in 2020 (Spahr, 2020). As noted above, Simon & Schuster's parent company is Paramount Global (formed through a merger of CBS Corporation and Viacom in 2019), a New York-based media and entertainment conglomerate. HarperCollins is owned by Rupert Murdoch's News Corp, a mass- and multimedia corporation which owns newspapers, television networks, and film production companies. Similarly, Hachette's parent company, Lagardère Publishing, is part of the Lagardère Group, a French corporation specialising in publishing, live entertainment, retail, radio, and media. Finally, Pan Macmillan is part of the German Holtzbrinck Publishing Group (HPG), a multinational group concentrated on publishing (a merger with Springer Science and Business Media in 2015 to create the British-German Springer Nature academic publishing group and also solidified HPG's position within the academic publishing sector (*Holtzbrinck Publishing Group and BC Partners*, 2015)). Each of the Big Five own significant numbers of imprints[3] (many of which were once small, independently run publishers in their own right) which manage individual lists of books and authors. Each imprint will also usually have its own focus or speciality (such as romance, horror, young adult, children).

Such mergers and acquisitions began in the early 1960s and erupted in force during the 1970s and 1980s. As Eric de Bellaigue argued in 1995: 'one can observe two major phases of publishing agglomeration since World War II. The first occurred in the late '60s, extending into the early '70s, and the second in the mid- '80s' (de Bellaigue, 1995, p. 7). For de Bellaigue, the earliest period of mergers and acquisitions was focused within the US, but in the late 1960s and early 1970s, a 'high level of corporate agglomeration' happened in the UK (de Bellaigue cites Pearson's purchase of Longman and Penguin as being one of the major cases) (de Bellaigue, 1995, p. 7). The so-called 'second wave' of mergers, in the 1980s, was 'a logical consequence of the progressive deregulation of currencies and markets generally' which saw more non-US/UK-based companies expanding their multinational reach (de Bellaigue, 1995, p. 7). However, by the late 1980s, 'the buying and selling of publishing houses on both sides of the Atlantic [was] sustained at a somewhat less frenetic level' (de Bellaigue, 1995, p. 7). Although de Bellaigue's analysis is of its time, it provides a useful indication of how the waves of mergers and acquisitions during the 1960s, 1970s, and 1980s were perceived somewhat contemporaneously. It also provides the backdrop to the publishing sectors' current position which sees most of the Big Five companies that dominate the industry—both through their international and economic heft and expansive imprint lists—sit under multinational parent companies. As Clark and Phillips note:

> In the UK, the 1980s were an important period of mergers and acquisitions that restructured the publishing industry and saw, like in the USA, its ownership largely transferred overseas. . . . The century's second decade was marked by further significant acquisitions. . . . The purchase of US publishers gives the mainland European publishers access to the world's largest and richest nation and the ability to grow quickly their dominant market share of English language book publishing worldwide.
>
> (Clark and Phillips, 2020, pp. 29–30)

This recent history of the consolidation of power and economy is both a symptom, and demonstration, of the Big Five's ability to dominate the consumer publishing market (and in some cases the Educational and Academic markets, which will be discussed below) in the UK. Independent publishers (or 'indie publishers') in the UK, on the other hand, can find it difficult to compete for exposure and opportunity. Independent publishers are typically small- to medium-sized enterprises (and often micro businesses) that work separately from a larger corporation or parent company. The Independent Publishers Guild (IPG), the UK's 'association for the thriving independent publishing sector in the UK and Ireland' (*About the IPG*, no date), state that they have 'more than 600 members working across trade, children's, academic, professional, educational and specialist publishing [and] share annual turnover of more than £1bn', which is around 15% of the industry's overall turnover (*About the IPG*, no date).[4] One of the biggest independent publishers, Bloomsbury, is a significant player in the consumer (and academic) market, but their exceptional status as one of the richest independent publishers in the UK (sales were £264.1 million, year end 2023, with £31.1 million of this being profit (*Latest results*, 2023)) is often credited to the fact that since 1997 they have published J.K. Rowling's Harry Potter series (Makortoff, 2022) and, in more recent years, have been the UK publisher of the bestselling American fantasy author Sarah J. Maas (Williams, 2022). To put Bloomsbury's success as an independent yet sizeable publisher (with offices in London, New York, Delhi, Sydney and Oxford) into context, the total consumer market value of the Independent Alliance, a group of 15 independent publishers in the UK, including Faber, Atlantic Books, Canongate, Granta Books, and Lonely Planet (see *Independent Alliance* (no date) for more), was £77.4 million in 2022 (Tivnan, 2023). However, Bloomsbury is an unusual example of a major indie consumer publisher as it also has a significant academic division, and the academic publishing market has its own unique publishing models and practices.

Academic Publishing

Upon the DCMS announcement of their latest figures that the UK Publishing industry was worth £6.9 billion in March 2023, the academic and former Bloomsbury editor David Barker tweeted: 'Does anyone else get mildly irritated whenever this number gets thrown around? (Given that over a third of that total comes from academic journals, which—no offence—aren't exactly the same thing [as consumer publishing])' (David Barker [@DavidBarker33], 2023). Barker's tweet highlighted the oft-overlooked disparity in economic market share within UK publishing sectors. Academic publishing is the most lucrative sector, making up over half—£3.5 billion—of the total revenue generated in the industry in 2022 (see Figure 1.3 for more details). This is despite a seemingly niche and highly specific target market and audience.

Academic publishers 'produce and distribute works of academic research and scholarship through non-fiction books, journals, textbooks, and online

UK Academic Market 2022		
	£	% increase or decrease in the previous year
Print		
Books	1,200,000,000	↑5
Print	668,000,000	↓3
Digital	514,000,000	↑17
Digital		
Journals	2,400,000,000	↑2
Print	309,000,000	↓5
Digital	2,000,000,000	↑3
Home market	1,000,000,000	↑2
Export market	2,500,000,000	↑3
Total	3,500,000,000	↑3

Figure 1.3 UK Academic Publishing Market Income 2022 (adapted from Publishers Association, 2023)

resources' (Publishers Association, no date). To expand on this, Samantha J. Rayner notes that:

> The term 'academic publishing' includes monographs, journals, editions of texts, higher education textbooks, and collections of essays, all of which have undergone some sort of peer review process. Simply put, the field covers the production and dissemination of knowledge and research, but, intricately involved with political issues around education and the value of the knowledge economy, accessibility, and status, it is, and always has been, a complex, innovative, and reflexive industry.
>
> (Rayner, 2019, p. 259)

The Publishers Association argue that 'Academic publishers pioneered digital publishing' with many publishers 'changing their model to publish Open Access (OA) content' (Publishers Association, no date). Rayner illustrates that the 'push towards OA is helped by policy', particularly in the UK, given that the Research Excellence Framework (REF)[5] requires all journal articles submitted for review to be Open Access (the OA model is a significant disruptor to traditional academic publishing business models and will be discussed in more detail below). Like other sectors, academic Publishing is also having to contend with the rapid developments in Artificial Intelligence (AI) and the various ways this can impact the production, dissemination, and reviewing of research (see Lawrence and Alam, 2022; Moorhouse, 2023; and, Waard, 2023, for more).

There are two types of Academic publishers: university presses and commercial publishers. The university press, as Rayner explains, is 'the most traditional' form of Academic publishing, as many of the most well-known university presses—such as Oxford University Press, Cambridge University Press, and Harvard University Press—have been around for decades (if not centuries) and have established recognition or prestige which often aligns with the reputation of the institution itself (Rayner, 2019, p. 263). University presses, particularly new and emerging ones, not only lean on the associations of expert knowledge and status from their institutions but can also rely on subsidisation and financial support from their respective institutions (and vice versa). In their 2021/22 Financial Statements, the University of Oxford noted that Oxford University Press (OUP) 'was able to transfer £140m to the rest of the University, to support a range of research, scholarship, and educational activities' (University of Oxford, 2022, p. 17). However, OUP also accounted for '£701.8m or 24% of the 2021/22 total expenditure' of the university (University of Oxford, 2022, p. 30). On the other hand, Liverpool University Press (LUP), which was founded in 1899 and claims to be the UK's third oldest university press (behind Oxford and Cambridge), receives no subsidiary support from the university (Liverpool University Press, no date). Writing in March 2022, LUP's CEO Anthony Cond explained the company's financial situation:

> [LUP] is an entirely self-funding, mission-driven publisher, receiving no operating subsidy whatsoever. Self-funding means careful financial

> planning and the need to generate a modest profit (a word university presses should use without embarrassment). Mission-driven means we're in it to disseminate scholarship and not to see a penny we generate taken out of the scholarly ecosystem. For last year that meant we turned over around £2.75 million and at first blush, before we decided to make some exceptional adjustments, the profit was around £60K.
>
> (Cond, 2022)

Cond's reflection demonstrates the tension that can exist for university presses which are perhaps torn between being 'mission-driven' in the distribution of research and scholarship and also earning a profit, whether for in-house investment or providing support to their affiliated institutions (as in the case with OUP).

This tension between profit and purpose is perhaps less of a concern for commercial Academic publishers, which, while also working in the realm of the dissemination of knowledge and research, need to ensure profitability. Because of this, the commercial market has arguably dictated the fraught business and production models that are now embedded within academic publishing. While there are examples of small, independently run Academic publishers in the UK (such as Emerald Group Publishing, Dunedin Academic Press, and Polity), others, much like the Big Five in the Consumer market, are part of multinational media companies. Rayner uses Elsevier, a 'global multimedia publishing business with over 20,000 products for educational and professional science and healthcare communities', as an example of an academic mega-publisher (Rayner, 2019, p. 265). Founded in 1880 in Amsterdam, Elsevier is a subsidiary of RELX, an information and analytics company based in London, which specialises in publishing in science, technology and medicine (STM). Like other multinational academic publishers, such as Taylor & Francis (a subsidiary of Informa, a £2 billion company that serves academic and business-to-business markets (Informa, no date)), or other major consumer publishers discussed previously, Elsevier's monolithic scale enables its influence within the academic publishing sector to expand. Rayner contends that,

> Elsevier often comes under attack for its business models, which help create massive profits: in 2010, Elsevier's scientific publishing arm reported profits of £724m on just over £2bn in revenue. This represents a 36 per cent margin—higher than Apple, Google, or Amazon posted that year. (Buranyi, 2017) This is a staggering amount; defendants of Elsevier underline that large amounts of that profit are ploughed back into the academic community, via initiatives like the Elsevier Foundation . . . but other researchers worry about the ethics of providing content, essentially for free, to a company that takes such a large profit from it.
>
> (Rayner, 2019, p. 265)

This point regarding the supply of 'free' content (by academics and researchers) which academic publishers then monetise and sell back to the research community via university libraries (and typically through expensive digital platforms, journal, or database subscription packages) is key to understanding the academic publishing market and its ability to demonstrate the kind of profits illustrated in Figure 1.3. Unlike consumer publishing, the payment of content creators in academic publishing (which in consumer publishing can also be minimal or non-existent, despite frequent sensational headlines about six-figure advances for authors) is not factored into the generation of content.

These publishing production and business models are inherently problematic and are exacerbated by processes of policy (such as the REF in the UK) and the requirements of academic career-building. Academic research requires time, funding, and expertise, and universities around the world strive to produce (or at least be seen to produce) world-leading research. Accordingly, the actual content published by Academic publishers comes largely from scholars and academics based in, or affiliated to, higher education institutions. Research time can be bought out through both internal (from within an institution's own reserves) and external funding support (from research councils like the Arts and Humanities Research Council (AHRC), the Economic and Social Research Council (ERSC), and Medical Research Council (MRC) in the UK), but research is also often completed alongside other responsibilities (such as teaching, marking, and administration). As a result, and due to the levels of competition within academic employment (in the UK and internationally), academic publishing benefits from a win-win situation of having a constant flow of content that is written, peer-reviewed, and edited for little to no cost and that they can (re)package and sell back to the very institutions employing the content creators. As Stephen Buranyi explains:

> Scientists create work under their own direction—funded largely by governments—and give it to publishers for free; the publisher pays scientific editors who judge whether the work is worth publishing and check its grammar, but the bulk of the editorial burden—checking the scientific validity and evaluating the experiments, a process known as peer review—is done by working scientists on a volunteer basis. The publishers then sell the product back to government-funded institutional and university libraries, to be read by scientists—who, in a collective sense, created the product in the first place.
>
> (Buranyi, 2017)

Some have argued that this business model is unsustainable. In response to such practices, in 2012, over 2,000 scholars protested against the mega-publisher Elsevier, signing an online pledge 'not to publish or do any editorial work for the company's journals, including refereeing papers' (Fischman, 2012). However, despite the fact that Elsevier was considered to be 'emblematic of an abusive publishing industry' (Fischman, 2012) and relationships with libraries began to deteriorate, this protest against exploitative publishing practices did not last: 'most libraries backed down and committed to Elsevier's contracts' and in '2012 and 2013, Elsevier posted profit margins of more than 40%' (Buranyi, 2017).

Academic publishing took another knock during the COVID-19 pandemic and national lockdowns through 2020 to 2021, due to the sudden lack of demand for print books (Comerford, 2020), but many publishers were able to swiftly utilise digital offerings and used this as an opportunity to further raise prices due to increased demand (Fazackerley, 2021). Furthermore, some maintain that the urgent need for expert knowledge and research about the outbreak of COVID-19 and potential causes, treatments, and cures, further exacerbated issues within academic publishing. In 2023, Clark noted that 'turbocharged scientific publishing' during the height of the pandemic in 2020 and 2021 led to editors feeling pressurised to publish the latest research, publishers loosening their peer review processes and shortening publication process timelines, and academic opportunism which saw researchers and institutions strive to become leaders in COVID-19 research (Clark, 2023, p. 689). During a time of scientific uncertainty this can be a positive, as it ensures the speedy dissemination of developments in understanding (although a number of hastily published research papers discussing potential treatments for COVID-19 were ultimately retracted due to misleading analyses and bad data (see Piller, 2021, for more)). However, Clark explains how the 'the gold rush to publish was simply an extension of the usual "publish or perish" culture' and that it has created a 'new citation elite and health leadership that will shape future funding and institutional priorities' (Clark, 2023, p. 689). In other words, researchers and institutions that were in the position to direct focus on pandemic-related research and outputs will benefit from the Academic publishing 'gold rush' for years to come. Accordingly, like other sectors within book publishing, and the Creative Industries more broadly, the Academic sector's profitability hinges on inherently problematic and exploitative business models.

Educational Publishing

According to the PA, educational publishing encompasses 'materials for educational markets such as primary and secondary schools; colleges and universities; and training programmes. This may include textbooks; indexes and abstracts; study guides; and digital resources and programmes' (Publishers Association, no date). As Figure 1.4 shows, the UK Education market (totalling £634 million in 2022) was particularly lucrative in the print export market but saw a downturn in the print home market. However, it is possible that this uptick was a result of the shift to predominantly online learning in 2020 and 2021, leading to less need and availability of print books for the home market in these years. Such numbers also demonstrate the profitability of the export market in educational publishing, which has been enabled by the UK's dominance in education markets around the world (which will be discussed in more detail below).

UK Education Market 2022		
	£	% increase or decrease in the previous year
Print (home market)	151,000,000	↓4
Digital (home market)	42,000,000	↑6
Print (export market)	388,000,000	↑388
Digital (export market)	53,000,000	↑16
Total income	634,000,000	↑16

Figure 1.4 UK Educational Publishing Market Income 2022 (adapted from Publishers Association, 2023)

Clark and Phillips split educational publishing into Schools Publishing and English Language Teaching (ELT) Publishing, explaining:

> Educational markets worldwide are subject to the influence of government, politics and regulations at the state, regional and local levels more than any other publishing sector. Generally speaking, the greater the amount of content prescription and regulatory control, the narrower the range of published material and that tends to favour large publishers over smaller publishers.
>
> (Clark and Phillips, 2020, p. 66)

Like the Consumer and Academic markets, this means that a handful of publishers who belong to media companies or publishing conglomerates dominate the sector as a result of major mergers and acquisitions over the years. Some of the largest Educational publishers include McGraw Hill, Houghton Mifflin Harcourt, and Pearson (once referred to as the 'Big Three' in educational publishing (Noonoo, 2012)). A brief overview of each of these publishers demonstrates why Educational publishing can be a particularly complex sector in terms of company formation and composition, as well as how it has taken the lead in making significant investments and expansions into digital technology in publishing.

McGraw Hill

McGraw Hill is a US-based publisher of educational materials and software for pre-school-aged children through to postgraduate level study. Established in 1888, the founders of McGraw Hill—James H. McGraw and John A. Hill—shared backgrounds in magazine and journal ownership, bringing together their knowledge of publishing production and publications for burgeoning industries (such as engineering) (*McGraw-Hill, Inc. | Encyclopedia.com*, no date). The company has continued to make significant acquisitions since the 1920s, focusing predominantly on the professional publishing and textbook markets (*The New York Times*, 1954), while also acquiring a number of financial services companies (*Business Wire*, 1997) and data analytics and consumer intelligence enterprises (McGraw-Hill, 2013). More recently, McGraw Hill has expanded into the online education market, purchasing Open University Press in the UK in 2002 (The Bookseller Editorial Team, 2002) and a number of digital learning platforms and 'personalised learning' services such as Redbird Advanced Learning in 2016 (McGraw-Hill, 2016) and Kidaptive, Inc. in 2021 (McGraw-Hill, 2021a). In 2022, the publisher also launched Sharpen, 'a mobile study app that delivers learning via a continuous content feed, bite-sized videos, swipeable study tools, and a personalized activity dashboard' (McGraw-Hill, no date). In 2021, McGraw Hill was bought by the private equity firm, Platinum Equity for $4.5 billion, with the Managing Director of Platinum Equity stating that 'McGraw Hill is a highly scalable enterprise with substantial opportunities for additional expansion', indicating that the publisher had been recognised as a business with promise for growth, particularly in digital products and tools (McGraw-Hill, 2021b).

Houghton Mifflin Harcourt

Also originating in the late nineteenth century, the foundation of what would later become Houghton Mifflin Harcourt was based on a number of significant mergers, acquisitions, and movement between companies and key individuals. While the original iteration of the publisher had focused on literary titles and authors, publishing Nathanial Hawthorne's *The Scarlet Letter* in 1850, several years of success following the establishment of an education department in 1891 made Houghton Mifflin Company (as it was then known) one of the largest educational publishers in the US by the 1920s. Although they continued to acquire literary publishers and titles into the mid-to-late twentieth century, Houghton Mifflin also continued to acquire major educational and professional publishers such as the educational branch of Rand McNally for $11.6 million in 1980; the textbook publisher McDougal, Littell & Company for $138 million in 1994; and D. C. Heath & Company educational publishing unit for $455 million in 1995 (Tabor, 1995). Similar to McGraw Hill, Houghton Mifflin Harcourt (as it has been known since the acquisition of Harcourt Education, Harcourt Trade, and Heinemann, from information-analytics company Reed Elsevier, in 2007 (RELX, 2007)) recognised the significance and profitability in the expansion of digital technology in educational publishing and acquired the 'educational Internet testing company' Virtual Learning Technologies for an undisclosed sum (*Business Wire*, 2000). What is more, after selling their consumer publishing portfolio in 2021 for $349 million to News Corps' Harper Collins (Trachtenberg and Cimilluca, 2021), Houghton Mifflin Harcourt was, like McGraw Hill, acquired by a private equity firm. In an announcement published in April 2022 about the deal, in which HMH (as it is has been known since 2024 (Caffrey, 2024)) is referred to as a 'learning technology company', the president and CEO of HMH Jack Lynch stated that this sale provides the company with the 'additional financial flexibility and opportunities for investment and expansion' required for the 'next phase of our long-term growth strategy' (HMH, 2022).

Pearson PLC

Based in the UK, Pearson PLC has evolved from its original incarnation, S Pearson & Son Ltd., a building and contractors business founded in 1844. As well as being a domestically and internationally renowned engineering company building major constructions in the UK, the US, and Mexico, S Pearson & Son (henceforth P&S) would also invest in coal mines, railways, aviation, and oil from the late 19th to the mid-twentieth century (Science Museum Group Collection, no date). Such investments were, however, complicated by the nationalisation of various industries, and the company would diversify and expand into media and newspapers from the mid-to-late twentieth century. By this time, P&S had acquired a number of regional newspapers, bought the *Financial Times* newspaper, and secured a 50% share in *The Economist* in 1957 (Science Museum Group Collection, no date). Aligning with the growth in mergers and acquisitions in publishing in the 1960s and 1970s more broadly (a pattern which has continued to the present day, see Thompson, 2012 and Clark and Phillips, 2020, for more), P&S acquired the publisher Longman (originally founded in 1724) in 1968, Penguin in 1970 (Pearson, 2013a), and the children's publisher Ladybird Books in 1972 ('Ladybird Books Ltd.', no date). In addition to unrelenting expansion in their consumer publishing assets (acquiring Frederick Warne in 1983 and Michael Joseph and Hamish Hamilton in 1985), Pearson (as they would be known from 1984) also continued their significant growth in the global education market. In 1988, Pearson purchased the science publisher Addison-Wesley, merging it with Longman to create Addison-Wesley Longman in 1994 (Hotten, 1994). Following the acquisition of Simon and Schuster's reference, education, and business and professional divisions from Viacom for $4.6 billion in 1998, Pearson would merge this with Addison-Wesley Longman to create Pearson Education, the 'world's leading education business' (Pearson, 2013a).[6] Pearson continued to make acquisitions into the 2000s and, much like their sector peers McGraw Hill and HMH, expanded into digital educational materials. In 2000, Pearson bought the US-based National Computer Systems Inc., the 'largest commercial testing and assessment company in the US' (Teather and Martinson, 2000) for $2.5 billion, and in 2005, they purchased AGS Publishing, another supplier of educational teaching and testing materials for the American market, for $270 million (The Independent, 2005). Pearson also acquired Connections Education which, at the time of the sale, operated a 'virtual school system' across 21 states in the US (Pearson, 2013b). As the parent company of Penguin since 1970, Pearson was involved in the major merger of Penguin and Random House in 2012. At the time of the merger, Pearson owned a 47% stake in the deal, with Random House parent company, Bertelsmann, holding the majority (*A new Penguin House*, 2012). Since 2012, Pearson has sold its entire share in PRH to Bertelsmann, selling 22% in July 2017 (Pearson, 2017) and the final 25% in 2020 (Penguin Random House, 2019). The sale saw Pearson move away from its consumer publishing ventures entirely, to focus on 'digital learning operations' (Reuters, 2019).

There are two key points that the origins and trajectories of these Educational publishers demonstrate with regards to the sector's position within publishing more broadly. First, it is clear that educational publishing has historically been viewed as one of the safer areas of publishing to invest in for individuals and companies developing portfolios of investment across different industries. Many of the key educational publishers that now dominate the market were founded during the era of industrial revolution in the UK, which was also a period of educational reform from which opportunities to manufacture and supply educational materials grew. Second, as educational publishers have expanded, merged, and consolidated, there has been a movement towards digitalisation within the sector, which has both driven, and responded to, demand. Some of this has been instigated by the shift to online learning following national lockdowns during the height of the COVID-19 pandemic, but, as the brief histories of a number of key educational publishers above show, expansions into the development of online learning environments and materials were happening in the 1990s and 2000s. And, as Clark and Phillips have noted, developments in digital educational materials require investment that only larger, multinational enterprises can afford:

> The migration to digital formats drives consolidation, not least in the ability enabled by size to invest in technology. Economies of scale along with the formation of large aggregations of content are critical in academic and STM publishing. The big players can afford to make the necessary large investments in online scientific journals and accompanying tools to aid researchers, and in building ebook collections for libraries. The larger the publisher's content and the greater their control over the intellectual property, the greater is the leverage of the aggregation. . . . It is argued by the large publishers that it is easier for academic libraries and their purchasing consortia to deal with just a few publishers and to use their platforms providing online content and services—rather than have to negotiate with dozens of publishers and intermediaries.
>
> (Clark and Phillips, 2020, p. 66)

This final point from Clark and Phillips is particularly prescient, given that Academic and Educational publishers were, according to some, able to take advantage of the move to teaching online during the pandemic, with both sectors being accused of 'price gouging' for access to online materials (Fazackerley, 2021).

What makes this summary of Educational publishing significant in a discussion of Publishing as a Creative Industry is that it demonstrates most clearly how the business, or industry, of publishing can work. Educational publishing in particular reveals how publishing can be approached from a standpoint of profitability over passion (which, as Chapter 3 explores, is a tension across the Creative Industries that is particularly pertinent in publishing), with many of the major educational publishers still operating today once belonging to portfolios of disparate industries. It also shows how shrewd investment in the sector has been over the centuries, making educational publishing a multi-billion pound (and dollar) sector.

This outline of the three key publishing sectors in the UK demonstrates how the major players in the industry approach the creative endeavour of writing and sharing information as an industrial process of mass producing a cultural product—the book—to insure commercial success. Additionally, and as will be discussed in the rest of this chapter, the global dominance of these multinational (although often UK and US concentrated) media and digital conglomerations leads to an Anglophonic literary and cultural dominance.

Number Matters

In 2020, 186,000 books were published in the UK (new and re-editions) (WIPO, 2022). Of the last reported data available (2013–2014), the UK was one of the top four countries which publish the highest number of titles per year. In 2013, the UK came fourth in the number of titles published, with 184,100. China was reported as publishing the most titles that year, 444,000 (going up to 448,000 in 2014) closely followed by the US with 304,912 in 2013 (there is no data available for the US in 2014). Yet, the International Publishers Association's (IPA's) 'Annual Report October 2014–October 2015' states that Brazil published 467,835 and 501,371 books in 2013 and 2014, respectively, indicating that the country is one of the highest producers of books in the world (IPA, 2015). However, the IPA report also notes that for Brazil, 'despite the growth in the total number of titles released, the number of new titles slightly decreased and, at the same time, the number of copies sold and revenue also decreased' ('Annual Report October 2014–October 2015', 2015, p. 18). Of the 501,371 books published in Brazil in 2014, for example, only 60,829 were new titles ('Annual Report October 2014–October 2015', 2015, p. 18) (there is no equivalent data regarding new titles provided in the report for the UK, the US, or China). The fact that UK news reports reflecting on the IPA report at the time focused on China, the US, and the UK's status as the 'top three' producers of books (see Flood, 2014; Moody, 2014) and omitted Brazil's position in the running may be a reflection on the fact that Brazil's publication figures are not demonstrative of significant growth in terms of revenue (despite publishing the most books in 2013, Brazil's revenue was €1.65 million compared to the UK's €4.5 million and the US' €24.2 million ('Annual Report October 2014–October 2015,' 2015, p. 17)) or publication of new titles. However, it may also be reflective of the perceived significance of the 'superpower' global political and economic dominance of the US and China as a means of more of a like-for-like comparison for the UK.

Another reason why there was a focus on the comparison between the UK and the US and China in terms of the number of books produced was the fact that it demonstrated that the UK published more books per capita than any other country. UK publishers releasing 184,000 titles in 2013 meant that they published '2,875 titles per million inhabitants', placing the UK '1,000-plus titles ahead of second-placed Taiwan and Slovenia (1,831)' (Flood, 2014). This indicates that the UK punches above its weight in book production. This is not only in terms of the domestic market but also internationally. The UK's export market in 2022 equated to £4.1 billion and was up by 8% in the previous year (Publishers Association, 2023). While there is no comparative export statistics for the US between 2020 and 2022, in 2018, US book publishers reported $1.06 billion in export revenue (Watson, 2021). The UK's apparent dominance over what is assumed to be the most likely competitor in the international English-language market is well established. As Nicola Wilson argues, '[t]he Anglophone book market was a large global business in the early twentieth century' and that '[t]he global trade in Anglophone literature at this time was dominated and fought over by British and American publishers' (Wilson, 2016, p. 18). Britain's so-called 'Empire markets' were, Wilson notes, 'of crucial importance to British publishing houses, both in terms of trade access and distribution', and the significance of the UK's imperial history in establishing the country as a global leader in Publishing will be discussed in more detail below (Wilson, 2016, p. 18).

Bringing this Anglophonic competition into the twenty-first century, in the 2008 *A Guide to the UK Publishing Industry*, published by the Publishers Association, Richardson and Taylor provide a comparative assessment of UK and US book exports by value across seven years between 1996 and 2007. While the US led the UK in exports by value in 1996, 1998, 2000, and 2002, Richardson and Taylor argue that 'since 2003 the UK has maintained a slight lead on the USA' (Richardson and Taylor, 2008, p. 13). Their data shows that in 2004, the UK's publishing export value was £1 billion as compared to the US' £949 million, a narrow difference of just under 9%. By 2007, this percentage difference had increased in the UK's favour to just over 12%, with the UK exports by value equalling £1.2 billion and US exports equalling £1 billion (Richardson and Taylor, 2008, p. 13). Richardson and Taylor acknowledge that '[t]he export picture is a complex one' and that success in the international market varies dramatically by publishing sectors and categories, as the discussion of the UK's Consumer, Academic, and Education markets herewith indicates (2008, p. 12). Success in an international market can also be 'strongly affected by the value of the point sterling against local currencies' (Richardson and Taylor, 2008, p. 12), and it is worth noting that the figures discussed in *A Guide to the UK Publishing Industry* come before the 2008 financial crash which affected economic markets around the world, as well as predating the UK's decision to leave the European Union in 2016 which has had an ongoing impact on the UK's economic growth (see Atkinson, 2022; and Baker, 2024 for more).

An Historical Advantage?

The UK's seemingly underdog status as an internationally influential Publishing powerhouse demands analysis. From the perspective of the industry and the UK government, this is, and historically has been, presented as a distinct feather in the cap of UK heritage and culture. The UK, home to world-renowned canonical writers like William Shakespeare, Charles Dickens, and Jane Austen, is frequently positioned as a forebearer in literature and publishing. The Guinness Book of World Records claims that Cambridge University Press, which received the Royal Letters Patent in 1534, is the oldest publisher in the world (Guinness World Records, no date) (although, Schwabe Verlag, a publisher founded in 1488 in Basel, Switzerland, also claims to hold the moniker of oldest publisher in the world (Schwabe Verlag, no date)). Indeed, it can be difficult to disentangle the realities of the UK Publishing industry, both historically and today, from idealised portrayals and hyperbolic accounts of the industry's past, present, and future. Richardson and Taylor's opening paragraphs in *A Guide to the UK Publishing Industry* provide an example of this. Subtitled 'The Historical Advantage', Richardson and Taylor provide an admirably brief summary of the printed word in the UK from the introduction to moveable type, to the industrialisation of the process via steam power which was, conveniently, 'pioneered in the UK' (2008, p. 1). The following quote provides an indication of the framing of the historical 'advantages' that enabled the modern success of the UK Publishing industry:

> In the UK the market was stimulated by the need for a literate workforce in an increasingly urbanised and industrialised society and by people's desire for the self-improvement and enjoyment that the printed work was so good at delivering. Globally it was encouraged by the use of English throughout the British Empire, and by the UK's leadership in international commerce and industrial technology. When the UK's superpower status began to wane in the late nineteenth and early twentieth centuries, the USA increasingly took up that role and assured the continued and increasing importance of *English as the international medium for commerce, culture, science and technology.*

> This delivered a powerful competitive advantage to the UK publishing industry, which it has been very successful in developing ever since.
>
> (emphasis in original, Richardson and Taylor, 2008, p. 1)

What is problematic in this overview-cum-homage to the originations of the foundations of the business of the printed word in the UK is the lack of interrogation of the economic, social, and political position of privilege that the UK possessed due to colonisation and the British Empire's oppressive rule. Rather than presenting the establishment of the English language as an 'international medium for commerce [and] culture', as a consequence of the British Empire's aggressive attempts to homogenise cultures and impose British ideals on colonised countries (see Pennycook, 2002; Tharoor, 2018; and, Ritter, 2021, for more), Richardson and Taylor suggest that it provided the foundation from which the UK could exploit a 'powerful competitive advantage' in Publishing (2008, p. 1). This is certainly the case, but as Wilson has noted, the key period of time during which 'the expansion of the international book trade in the late nineteenth-century [that] went hand-in-hand with developments in global communications technologies and transportation' and enabled the UK to establish such command in book production and trade, was also the period (1900–1940) at which the 'British Empire was at its geographical height . . . and especially the years between the two World Wars' (Wilson, 2016, p. 18). The political, economic, cultural, and geographic dominance facilitated by British imperial rule 'gave British publishers important trade access to the huge Anglophone reading and book-buying markets of Australia and New Zealand, India and Canada, as well as many other territories and "Dominions."' (Wilson, 2016, p. 18), and the UK Publishing industry was determined in preserving this 'monopoly of trade' to safeguard publishers, so much so that it was 'a substantial part of the day-to-day work of the publishers trade body [the Publishers' Association of Great Britain & Ireland]' (now known as the Publishers Association) (Wilson, 2016, p. 18). The impact of this imperial supremacy is still evident today. The Publishers Association's online 'Export Toolkit' identifies South Africa as lying in the 'top five or six territories in terms of turnover' for UK publishers with a 'mature export operation' (Publishers Association, 2019b). The toolkit also notes that one of the core areas for UK Educational publishers is 'International publishing for specific local curricula outside the UK/For example, Jamaica, Trinidad & Tobago, Botswana, Kenya', all of which are former British colonies which achieved independence in the 1960s (Publishers Association, 2019a). The UK's monopoly in such territories continues, but in recent years, the US has attempted to seek rights in territories that are 'traditionally the preserve of UK publishers', with India being the 'top of the contested territories, while Singapore, Malaysia and South Africa are also significant' (Allen, 2010). Reflecting on this, Thomas Abraham, the Managing Director of Hachette India, 'stressed the importance of the "colonial legacy" in terms of British spelling, cover design and marketing' in these markets, arguing that '[l]eaving aside the negatives of colonial history, it does seem logical that the UK product fits more naturally—it is the natural flow' (Allen, 2010). Abraham thus reveals the enduring legacy of the British Empire upon international book publishing well into the twenty-first century.

To return to Richardson and Taylor, their correlation, if not analysis, of UK Publishing, the legacies of Empire, and the opportunities it still delivers raises two points worth examining. First, their uncritical reading exemplifies the thorny undercurrent of publishing in the UK that exists to this day. The success of the industry, like many other commercial and creative industries, is dependent on cultural and economic dominance, which is typically gained through the exploitation of labour and forceful cultural ascendency. This is illustrated not only by the industry's reportedly poor remuneration of workers but also by the compensation and support of authors: a survey of writers in the UK in 2022 found that there was a 'decline in median (typical) earnings from self-employed writing among primary occupation authors of 38.2% (in real terms)' (Thomas et al., 2022, p. 7), with 'Primary occupation authors earn[ing] a median income of £7,000 in 2022' (Thomas et al., 2022, p. 22). This leads the authors of the report to conclude that 'Writing in itself cannot sustain an income that is consistent with a minimum wage [in the UK]' (Thomas et al., 2022, p. 22). The disparity between the Publishing industry's outward overall economic success and the unsustainability of the industry for its workforce (including authors) will be discussed in more detail in Chapter 2.

The second, and related, issue that Richardson and Taylor's hyperbolic description of the originations of the UK publishing industry reveals is the inherent neoliberalism of contemporary publishing that has been sustained by the neoliberal economic policies and sociocultural discourses of successive UK governments since the 1970s. Like Turner in 1988, Richardson and Taylor tie the creative dynamism of the UK to the boom in private businesses and enterprises in the UK during the 1980s and 1990s. This consolidation and association between economics, business, and culture were deliberately fostered by the UK government in the latter half of the twentieth century, and, as will be examined throughout this book, this sociocultural, political, and economic context is crucial to understanding book publishing in the UK and the inherent tensions between culture and commerce it leads to.

As this chapter has illustrated, the UK Publishing industry is a vast and complex sector that has continually responded to commercial demands and changes. Like other creative industries, which have seen consolidation and procurement lead to market dominance by fewer and fewer conglomerates (see Doyle, 2023; Penick, 2020; and FilmTake, 2024), certain sectors and aspects of book publishing in the UK have maintained a particular power within the global publishing market. Crucially, the origins of such dominance have been influenced, and made possible, by broader sociopolitical, historical and cultural developments, as well as economic changes, on a domestic and international scale. However, as the following chapters of this book demonstrate, the Publishing industry's status as a multi-billion pound (and dollar) Creative Industry has not only been enabled by the problematic business practices detailed above, but has also been bolstered by the perpetuation of an idealised view of work in the industry, as well as the presumed (high) cultural value of books as a form of cultural production.

Notes

1 There have, however, been enduring problems caused by the pandemic, including reduced capacity at international book fairs (Anderson, 2022), reports of major publishing events leading to a rise of infections (Nathan, 2022), and authors reporting a continued loss of earnings and opportunities (Comerford, 2022). Not to mention the concerns of some that the industry has been too quick to return to in-person events, with a group of campaigners for disability rights and inclusion in the arts calling for literary festivals to maintain hybrid options for attendance so as not to disadvantage people who remain vulnerable to significant harm from the coronavirus (Bayley, 2022).

2 The terms 'Consumer' and 'Trade' are often used interchangeably to refer to the sectors within the industry that are focused on the general reading public (or consumers). As this discussion refers to the Publishers Association's 'A Year in Books' report which uses the term 'Consumer', this term is favoured throughout this chapter.

3 While the total number of imprints for each of the Big Five is difficult to determine, PRH claims to have over 300 imprints and brands, Hachette over 200, and HarperCollins over 120.

4 It is worth noting that the IPG's membership cannot be taken as an indication as to how many independent publishers are currently working in the UK, as some indie publishers may not be members, and some members may run more than one press.

5 The REF is a research assessment exercise founded in 2014 and conducted every six years which sees the four UK higher education funding bodies (Research England, the Scottish Funding Council, the Higher Education Funding Council for Wales, and the Department for the Economy, Northern Ireland) undertake an 'expert review' of academic research outputs across the UK (for more, see: REF, no date).

6 Although, as Jim Milliot explains, this deal was not as simple as first reported:

> Pearson paid a total of $4.6 billion for the [Simon and Schuster] assets, and sold the reference, business, and professional groups to [private equity firm] Hicks, Muse for $1 billion, leaving Pearson with a bill of $3.6 billion for the school, higher education, and international groups.
>
> (Milliot, 2022)

References

About the IPG. (no date). Available at: https://www.independentpublishersguild.com/IPG/IPG/About_the_IPG/About-the-IPG.aspx (Accessed: 19 June 2023).

Allen, K. (2010) 'US chips away at UK export markets', *The Bookseller*, 20 June. Available at: https://www.thebookseller.com/news/us-chips-away-uk-export-markets (Accessed: 16 May 2023).

Anderson, P. (2022) *Frankfurter Buchmesse Aims for 70% of Its Pre-Pandemic Size, Publishing Perspectives*. Available at: https://publishingperspectives.com/2022/09/frankfurter-buchmesse-aims-for-70-percent-of-its-pre-pandemic-size/ (Accessed: 21 June 2023).

Atkinson, A. (2022) 'Brexit has made UK less open and competitive, study finds', *Bloomberg.com*, 21 June. Available at: https://www.bloomberg.com/news/articles/2022-06-21/brexit-has-made-uk-less-open-and-competitive-study-finds (Accessed: 18 December 2024).

Baker, T. (2024) 'Brexit: New report suggests UK £311bn worse off by 2035 due to leaving EU', *Sky News*, 11 January. Available at: https://news.sky.com/story/brexit-new-report-suggests-uk-311bn-worse-off-by-2035-due-to-leaving-eu-13046256 (Accessed: 18 December 2024).

Bayley, S. (2022) 'Campaigners call on literary festivals to find ways to retain digital access', *The Bookseller*. Available at: https://www.thebookseller.com/news/campaigners-call-on-literary-festivals-to-find-ways-to-retain-digital-access (Accessed: 21 June 2023).

Blackwell, H. (2022) 'Biden antitrust enforcers take aim at mergers and acquisitions: Legal Updates', 23 February. Available at: https://www.huschblackwell.com/newsandinsights/biden-antitrust-enforcers-take-aim-at-mergers-and-acquisitions (Accessed 19 March 2025).

Bloomsbury. (2023) 'Latest results—Corporate and investor relations—Bloomsbury.com', *Bloomsbury Publishing plc*. Available at: https://www.bloomsbury-ir.co.uk/financial/f_latest (Accessed: 19 June 2023).

The Bookseller Editorial Team. (2002) *McGraw-Hill buys Open UP, The Bookseller*. Available at: https://www.thebookseller.com/news/2002-mcgraw-hill-buys-open (Accessed: 16 October 2024).

The Bookseller Editorial Team. (2023) 'Thirst for 'solutions-focused' books as non-fiction plateaus', *The Bookseller*. Available at: https://www.thebookseller.com/news/thirst-for-solutions-focused-books-as-non-fiction-plateaus (Accessed: 24 October 2024).

Buranyi, S. (2017) 'Is the staggeringly profitable business of scientific publishing bad for science?', *The Guardian*, 27 June. Available at: https://www.theguardian.com/science/2017/jun/27/profitable-business-scientific-publishing-bad-for-science (Accessed: 20 June 2023).

Business Wire. (1997) 'The McGraw-Hill companies to acquire micropal', 16 October. Available at: https://web.archive.org/web/20181028025225/https://www.thefreelibrary.com/The+McGraw-Hill+Companies+to+Acquire+Micropal-a019861914.

Business Wire. (2000) 'Houghton Mifflin company acquires virtual learning technologies; acquisition extends riverside publishing's reach into web-based testing', 8 May. Available at: https://advance.lexis.com/document/?pdmfid=1516831&crid=c8baea6f-f380-4451-84eb-6a689e51ae3c&pddocfullpath=%2Fshared%2Fdocument%2Fnews%2Furn%3AcontentItem%3A4070-D3H0-00RH-416B-00000-00&pdcontentcomponentid=7924&pdteaserkey=sr0&pditab=allpods&ecomp=h6yyk&ea

rg=sr0&prid=baac37df-4862-4d2d-90b9-6a1faae14299 (Accessed: 21 October 2024).

Cader, M. (2013) 'DOJ Approves Penguin Random House merger', *Publishers Lunch*. Available at: https://lunch.publishersmarketplace.com/2013/02/doj-approves-penguin-random-house-merger/ (Accessed: 19 June 2023).

Caffrey, M. (2024) 'Houghton Mifflin Harcourt rebrands as simply 'HMH'', *Marketbrief*. Available at: https://marketbrief.edweek.org/strategy-operations/houghton-mifflin-harcourt-rebrands-as-simply-hmh/2024/07 (Accessed: 22 October 2024).

Carter, S. (2012) 'Authors Guild asks for "close scrutiny" of Penguin Random House merger', *Quill and Quire*, 5 November. Available at: https://quillandquire.com/book-news/2012/11/05/authors-guild-asks-for-close-scrutiny-of-penguin-random-house-merger/ (Accessed: 19 June 2023).

Clark, G. and Phillips, A. (2020) *Inside Book Publishing*. 6th edn. Oxon: Routledge.

Clark, J. (2023) 'How covid-19 bolstered an already perverse publishing system', *BMJ*, 380, p. 689. Available at: https://doi.org/10.1136/bmj.p689.

Comerford, R. (2020) 'Challenges ahead', as university presses adapt to Covid changes', *The Bookseller*. Available at: https://www.thebookseller.com/news/academic-presses-have-signifcant-challenges-ahead-publishers-say-1207933 (Accessed: 21 June 2023).

Comerford, R. (2022) 'Authors still 'suffering badly' from pandemic, SoA survey finds', *The Bookseller*. Available at: https://www.thebookseller.com/news/authors-still-suffering-badly-from-pandemic-soa-survey-finds (Accessed: 21 June 2023).

Cond, A. (2022) 'How shall I value a university press? Let me count the ways', *Liverpool University Press Blog*, 16 March. Available at: https://liverpooluniversitypress.blog/2022/03/16/how-shall-i-value-a-university-press-let-me-count-the-ways/ (Accessed: 20 June 2023).

David Barker [@DavidBarker33]. (2023) 'Does anyone else get mildly irritated whenever this number gets thrown around? (Given that over a third of that total comes from academic journals, which—no offence—aren't exactly the same thing. . .)' https://t.co/bWJpSU5Tes', *Twitter*. Available at: https://twitter.com/DavidBarker33/status/1631256869367951361 (Accessed: 20 June 2023).

de Bellaigue, E. (1995) 'Mergers, acquisitions and takeovers in publishing: Why they go on, and on, and will go on', *LOGOS*, 6(1), pp. 6–15. Available at: https://doi.org/10.2959/logo.1995.6.1.6.

Doyle, G. (2023) *Television Production, International Trade and Pressures to Consolidate*. Available at: https://pec.ac.uk/policy_briefing_entr/television-production-international-trade-and-pressures-to-consolidate/ (Accessed: 11 December 2024).

Fazackerley, A. (2021) '"Price gouging from Covid": Student ebooks costing up to 500% more than in print', *The Guardian*, 29 January. Available at: https://www.theguardian.com/education/2021/jan/29/price-gouging-from-covid-student-ebooks-costing-up-to-500-more-than-in-print (Accessed: 21 June 2023).

FilmTake. (2024) 'The Media Conundrum: A complex interplay of conso lidation, mergers, and streaming misfortunes', *FilmTake*, 24 January.

Available at: https://www.filmtake.com/distribution/the-media-conundrum-a-complex-interplay-of-consolidation-mergers-and-streaming-misfortunes/ (Accessed: 11 December 2024).

Fischman, J. (2012) 'As journal boycott grows, Elsevier defends its practices', *The Chronicle of Higher Education*, 31 January. Available at: https://www.chronicle.com/article/as-journal-boycott-grows-elsevier-defends-its-practices/ (Accessed: 20 June 2023).

Flood, A. (2014) 'UK publishes more books per capita than any other country, report shows', *The Guardian*, 22 October. Available at: https://www.theguardian.com/books/2014/oct/22/uk-publishes-more-books-per-capita-million-report (Accessed: 16 May 2023).

The Guardian. (2022) 'Paramount scraps $2.2bn sale of Simon & Schuster publishing to Penguin', 21 November. Available at: https://www.theguardian.com/books/2022/nov/21/penguin-simon-schuster-merger-abandoned-paramount-bertelsmann (Accessed: 19 June 2023).

Guinness World Records. (no date) *Oldest Publisher, Guinness World Records*. Available at: https://www.guinnessworldrecords.com/world-records/67257-oldest-publisher (Accessed: 16 May 2023).

HMH. (2022) *Houghton Mifflin Harcourt Successfully Completes Sale to Veritas Capital*. Available at: https://www.hmhco.com/about-us/press-releases/houghton-mifflin-harcourt-successfully-completes-sale-to-veritas-capital (Accessed: 22 October 2024).

Holtzbrinck Publishing Group and BC Partners. (2015) 'Holtzbrinck Publishing Group and BC Partners announce agreement to merge majority of Mac millan Science and Education with Springer Science+Business Media', *Springer Nature Group*. Available at: https://www.springer.com/gp/about-springer/media/press-releases/corporate/holtzbrinck-publishing-group-and-bc-partners-announce-agreement-to-merge-majority-of-macmillan-science-and-education-with-springer-science-business-media/43672 (Accessed: 19 June 2023).

Hotten, R. (1994) 'Pearson breaks up book arm in restructuring', *The Independent*. Available at: https://www.independent.co.uk/news/business/pearson-breaks-up-book-arm-in-restructuring−1450185.html (Accessed: 22 October 2024).

The Independent. (2005) 'Pearson's $270m teaching deal taps into growing specialist market', *The Independent*, 23 June. Available at: https://www.independent.co.uk/news/business/news/pearson-s-270m-teaching-deal-taps-into-growing-specialist-market−5346147.html (Accessed: 22 October 2024).

Independent Alliance. (no date) *Faber*. Available at: https://www.faber.co.uk/independent-alliance/ (Accessed: 19 June 2023).

Informa. (no date) *What We Do*. Available at: https://www.informa.com/about-us/what-we-do/ (Accessed: 20 June 2023).

IPA. (2015) *Annual Report October 2014—October 2015*. Geneva: International Publishers Association.

'Ladybird Books Ltd.' (no date). Available at: https://collections.reading.ac.uk/special-collections/collections/ladybird-books-ltd-archive-and-library/ (Accessed: 22 October 2024).

Lawrence, R. and Alam, S. (2022) 'AI paper mills and image generation require a co-ordinated response from academic publishers', *Impact of Social Sciences*, 15 December. Available at: https://blogs.lse.ac.uk/impactofsocialsciences/2022/12/15/ai-paper-mills-and-image-generation-require-a-co-ordinated-response-from-academic-publishers/ (Accessed: 20 June 2023).

Liverpool University Press. (no date) *About Us, Liverpool University Press*. Available at: https://www.liverpooluniversitypress.co.uk/pages/about/ (Accessed: 20 June 2023).

Makortoff, K. (2022) 'Harry Potter publisher Bloomsbury reports record sales amid reading boom', *The Guardian*, 15 June. Available at: https://www.theguardian.com/business/2022/jun/15/harry-potter-publisher-bloomsbury-reports-record-sales-amid-reading-boom-covid (Accessed: 19 June 2023).

McGraw-Hill. (2013) "Investors: News releases—The McGraw-Hill Companies—The McGraw-Hil', *Archive.PH*. Available at: https://archive.ph/RQO4R (Accessed: 16 October 2024).

McGraw-Hill. (2016) *McGraw-Hill Acquires Redbird Advanced Learning, A Digital Personalized Learning Provider for K*. Available at: https://www.mheducation.com/news-insights/press-releases/mcgraw-hill-education-acquires-redbird-learning.html (Accessed: 16 October 2024).

McGraw-Hill. (2021a) *McGraw Hill Acquires Kidaptive, an Adaptive and Personalized Learning Company*. Available at: https://www.mheducation.com/news-insights/press-releases/mcgraw-hill-acquires-kidaptive-inc.html (Accessed: 16 October 2024).

McGraw-Hill. (2021b) *Platinum Equity to Acquire McGraw Hill from Apollo Funds for $4.5 Billion*. Available at: https://www.mheducation.com/news-insights/press-releases/platinum-equity-to-acquire-mcgraw-hill-from-apollo.html (Accessed: 16 October 2024).

McGraw-Hill. (no date) *About Us, About McGraw Hill UK & Europe*. Available at: https://www.mheducation.co.uk/about-us (Accessed: 16 October 2024).

McGraw-Hill, Inc. (no date) 'McGraw-Hill, Inc.', *Encyclopedia.com*. Available at: https://www.encyclopedia.com/books/politics-and-business-magazines/mcgraw-hill-inc (Accessed: 16 October 2024).

Milliot, J. (2022) 'Over the past 25 years, the big publishers got bigger—and fewer', *PublishersWeekly.com*. Available at: https://www.publishersweekly.com/pw/by-topic/industry-news/publisher-news/article/89038-over-the-past-25-years-the-big-publishers-got-bigger-and-fewer.html (Accessed: 22 October 2024).

Moody, O. (2014) 'Britain holds world title in book publishing', *The Times*, 23 October. Available at: https://www.thetimes.co.uk/article/britain-holds-world-title-in-book-publishing-722q8lwmtcs (Accessed: 15 May 2023).

Moorhouse, S. (2023) 'Preparing for academic AI', *The Bookseller*. Available at: https://www.thebookseller.com/comment/preparing-for-academic-ai (Accessed: 20 June 2023).

Nathan, L. (2022) 'Covid outbreak hits U.K. Book business following London book fair', *PublishersWeekly.com*. Available at: https://www.publishersweekly.com/pw/by-topic/international/london-book-fair/article/89025-covid-outbreak-hits-u-k-book-business-following-lbf.html (Accessed: 21 June 2023).

A New Penguin House. (2012). Available at: https://pearsonblog.campaign-server.co.uk/2012/10/ (Accessed: 23 October 2024).

The New York Times. (1954) 'Blakiston Books sold; McGraw-Hill acquires medical subsidiary of Doubleday', 18 October. Available at: https://www.nytimes.com/1954/10/18/archives/blakiston-books-sold-mcgrawhill-acquires-medical-subsidiary-of.html (Accessed: 16 October 2024).

Noonoo, S. (2012) 'How 'Big Three' publishers are approaching iPad textbooks', *THE Journal*. Available at: https://thejournal.com/Articles/2012/11/08/How-big-three-publishers-are-approaching-their-ipad-textbooks.aspx (Accessed: 16 October 2024).

Pearson. (2013a) *Our History*. Available at: https://web.archive.org/web/20131015023257/http://www.pearson.com/about-us/our-history.html (Accessed: 22 October 2024).

Pearson. (2013b) *Pearson Acquires Connections Education*. Available at: https://web.archive.org/web/20130620145444/http://www.pearson.com/news/2011/september/pearson-acquires-connections-education.html (Accessed: 23 October 2024).

Pearson. (2017) 'Pearson agrees to sell a 22% stake in Penguin Random House to Bertelsmann and recapitalise the business generating total net proceeds of approximately $1 billion', *Pearson plc*. Available at: https://plc.pearson.com/en-GB/news-and-insights/news/pearson-agrees-sell-22-stake-penguin-random-house-bertelsmann-and (Accessed: 23 October 2024).

Penguin Random House. (2019) 'Bertelsmann acquires full ownership of Penguin Random House', *penguinrandomhouse.com*. Available at: https://global.penguinrandomhouse.com/announcements/bertelsmann-acquires-full-ownership-of-penguin-random-house/ (Accessed: 23 October 2024).

Penick, B. (2020) 'Post-pandemic music industry predictions: The consolidation of power', *Forbes*. Available at: https://www.forbes.com/sites/brianpenick/2020/05/29/post-pandemic-music-industry-predictions-the-consolidation-of-power/ (Accessed: 11 December 2024).

Pennycook, A. (2002) *English and the Discourses of Colonialism*. Routledge.

Piller, C. (2021) *Many Scientists Citing two Scandalous COVID-19 Papers Ignore Their Retractions*. Available at: https://www.science.org/content/article/many-scientists-citing-two-scandalous-covid-19-papers-ignore-their-retractions (Accessed: 14 October 2024).

Publishers Association. (2019a) 'In-depth toolkit: Education publishing | Export Toolkit', 5 March. Available at: https://www.publishing-export.org.uk/resourceins/in-depth-toolkit-education-publishing/ (Accessed: 16 May 2023).

Publishers Association. (2019b) 'South Africa | Export Toolkit', 21 February. Available at: https://www.publishing-export.org.uk/countries/south-africa/ (Accessed: 16 May 2023).

Publishers Association. (2023) 'A year in publishing', *Publishers Association.* Available at: https://www.publishers.org.uk/publications/a-year-in-publishing/ (Accessed: 16 May 2023).

Publishers Association. (no date) 'Learn about the industry', *Publishers Association.* Available at: https://www.publishers.org.uk/about-publishing/learn-about-the-industry/ (Accessed: 16 May 2023).

Publisher's Weekly. (2013) 'Random House, Penguin merger completed', 1 July.

Rayner, S.J. (2019) 'Academic Publishing', In *The Oxford Handbook of Publishing.* Oxford: Oxford University Press, pp. 259–273.

REF. (no date) *What is the REF?—REF 2021, Higher Education Funding Council for England.* Available at: https://www.ref.ac.uk/about-the-ref/what-is-the-ref/ (Accessed: 20 June 2023).

RELX. (2007) *Sale of Harcourt to Houghton Mifflin.* Available at: https://www.relx.com/media/press-releases/archive/16-07-2007 (Accessed: 22 October 2024).

Reuters. (2019) 'Pearson exits consumer publishing with Penguin Random House disposal', *CNBC.* Available at: https://www.cnbc.com/2019/12/18/pearson-exits-consumer-publishing-with-penguin-random-house-disposal.html (Accessed: 23 October 2024).

Richardson, P. and Taylor, G. (2008) *A Guide to the UK Publishing Industry.* Publishers Association.

Ritter, C. (2021) *Imperial Encore: The Cultural Project of the Late British Empire.* University of California Press.

Schwabe Verlag. (no date) 'The Publisher', *Schwabe Verlag.* Available at: https://schwabe.ch/ (Accessed: 16 May 2023).

Science Museum Group Collection. (no date) *S Pearson & Son Ltd.* Available at: https://collection.sciencemuseumgroup.org.uk/people/ap10/s-pearson-son-ltd (Accessed: 22 October 2024).

Spahr, W. (2020) 'BMG owner Bertelsmann wraps 100% takeover of Penguin Random House', *Billboard,* 2 April. Available at: https://www.billboard.com/music/music-news/bertelsmann-purchase-penguin-random-house-9349594/#! (Accessed: 19 June 2023).

Tabor, M.B.W. (1995) 'Houghton Mifflin to buy publisher D. C. Heath', *The New York Times,* 26 September, p. 9.

Teather, D. and Martinson, J. (2000) 'Pearson buys US net education firm', *The Guardian,* 1 August. Available at: https://www.theguardian.com/media/2000/aug/01/pearson.mondaymediasection (Accessed: 22 October 2024).

Tharoor, S. (2018) *Inglorious Empire: What the British Did to India.* Penguin UK.

Thomas, A., Battisti, M. and Kretschmer, M. (2022) *UK Authors' Earnings and Contracts 2022: A Survey of 60,000 Writers.* CREATe, University of Glasgow.

Thompson, J. (2012) *Merchants of Culture: The Publishing Business in the Twenty-First Century.* Cambridge: Polity Press.

Tivnan, T. (2023) 'Big Four's market share contracts as mid-range publishers make hay', *The Bookseller.* Available at: https://www.thebookseller.com/spotlight/spotlight/big-fours-market-share-contracts-as-mid-range-publishers-make-hay (Accessed: 19 June 2023).

Trachtenberg, J.A. and Cimilluca, D. (2021) 'News Corp to Buy Houghton Mifflin Harcourt's consumer-publishing arm for $349 million', *Wall Street*

Journal, 28 March. Available at: https://www.wsj.com/articles/news-corp-nears-deal-to-buy-houghton-mifflin-harcourt-s-consumer-publishing-arm-11616970992 (Accessed: 21 October 2024).

University of Oxford. (2022) *University of Oxford: Financial Statements 2021/22*. University of Oxford. Available at: https://www.ox.ac.uk/about/organisation/finance-and-funding (Accessed: 20 June 2023).

Waard, A. de. (2023) 'Guest post—AI and scholarly publishing: A view from three experts', *The Scholarly Kitchen*. Available at: https://scholarlykitchen.sspnet.org/2023/01/18/guest-post-ai-and-scholarly-publishing-a-view-from-three-experts/ (Accessed: 20 June 2023).

Watson, A. (2021) 'Book publishing in the U.S.—export revenue 2010–2018', *Statista*. Available at: https://www.statista.com/statistics/511003/book-publishing-export-revenue-usa/ (Accessed: 16 May 2023).

Williams, H. (2022) 'Bloomsbury ups profit outlook again after success of Sarah Maas's bestseller', *The Independent*, 30 March. Available at: https://www.independent.co.uk/business/bloomsbury-ups-profit-outlook-again-after-success-of-sarah-maas-s-bestseller-b2046990.html (Accessed: 19 June 2023).

Wilson, N.L. (ed.). (2016) *The Book World: Selling and Distributing British Literature, 1900–1940*. BRILL.

WIPO. (2022) *The Global Publishing Industry in 2020*. Geneva: World Intellectual Property Organization.

2 Searching for 'Diversity' in Publishing (and the Creative Industries)

It can seem as though concerns surrounding representation, inclusion, and access into the Creative Industries is a particularly current phenomenon, instigated, perhaps, by broader sociocultural and political liberalisation and progression in the UK which calls for responses and changes to systemic inequities and inequality.[1] Indeed, debates regarding the key trends and issues pertaining to the Creative Industries (both as an entire sector and the specific industries within it) have swirled—both in policy reports and documents and academic literature—over the past 20 to 30 years. UK publishers in particular seem to have been aware of potential issues and risks as far back as the late 1980s. In *Publishing—The Future* (1988), a book of essays by key publishing figures of the time, several contributors highlight, or hint at, some of the problems within the industry that continue to impact it to this day. Much of the discussion in the book relates to changes in business models and structures of the industry, as well as reflections on the globalisation of the industry instigated by the emergence of major conglomerate publishers and multinational media companies; Peter Owen, the editor and publisher of the book, states in his introduction: 'Publishers can survive only if they think in global terms' (Owen, 1988, p. 8). Essays in the collection also reflect on the problematic 'romantic air' of the industry (which will be discussed in more detail in Chapter 3). However, others comment on the impact of conservative policies which inhibit public funding and subsidy for access to books, specifically through library cuts, as well as the difficulties of entry into, and inclusion within, the industry, particularly for women and individuals who do not have access to personal capital. For example in her essay contemplating 'Publishing as a Career', Marion Boyars, one of 'the first women publishers' in the UK (Owen, 1988, p. 126) not only reflects on the benefit of existing financial support or wealth to facilitate entering the industry but also comments on the differing opportunities within the industry for men and women. On the entrepreneurial spirit needed to enter and succeed in the industry, Boyars notes:

> Many young women—and men—have over the years consulted me about their publishing careers. To follow my example is not open to

DOI: 10.4324/9781003187905-3

> many, not only because of lack of capital (or lack of courage to raise it), but mainly because you need a certain type of mentality to become an entrepreneur in this field. Most people see work in terms of employment which supplies an instant context, financial security and the freedom to move around. The publishing entrepreneur, often with some initial experience of employment, who creates his own context and exposes his taste to public critical appraisal, is willing to forgo security (at least for a time), and weighs up freedom to move jobs against freedom of self-determination.
>
> (Owen, 1988, pp. 120–121)

While Boyars acknowledges that her specific circumstances—having capital to invest in a publishing company to enter the industry—are not available to everyone, she also indicates that individuals who want to work in publishing must accept, or at least expect, financial (and perhaps role) insecurity and a lack of freedom in deciding where they may work and live. This reflects two of the key problems that remain—well over 30 years later—central to current inequities and lack of access within the publishing industry (and Creative Industries more broadly), namely: barriers to access for individuals from lower levels of personal or familial wealth, and the centralisation of the Creative Industries in specific areas of the country, namely London.

On gender and representation within the publishing industry, Boyars is simultaneously optimistic and cynical. She argues that women are increasingly present in publishing, although admits that entry into the sector for women 'often means starting as a secretary, and usually remaining one' (although, women can find themselves 'promoted into a more responsible and thus more satisfying position' if they 'take good notes' and show an interest in the 'mechanics' as well as the 'literary aspects of publishing') (Owen, 1988, p. 122). Indeed, Boyars acknowledges the distinct lack of progression for women in publishing, arguing:

> [A] female *corporation* executive is still such a rarity that you can count their numbers *worldwide* on *primary* public company publishing boards on one hand. I think the reason for this is mental and subtle: men feel uncomfortable with women in positions of competitive power, even though many subscribe today to the idea that women should be in decision-making positions. . . . So the defensive male trick against that inclusion of women (apart from the claim that there are not any *good* ones) has been the creation of two boards: the *executive* board without women that makes *business*, i.e. the *real* (money) decision, and the *working* board which makes publishing decision and on to which some women are invited, but even that is a new development.
>
> (Owen, 1988, p. 121)

Problematic generalisations aside and bearing in mind that the broader context of women working in corporate roles in the 1980s was likely novel in many industries and the fact that the UK Equal Pay Act only came into force in 1970 (despite the TUC (Trades Union Congress) calling for it in the nineteenth century (Francis-Devine and Ferguson, 2020)), Boyars' reflections on gender disparity within publishing remain relevant even today. Specifically, while the gender balance within the industry has undoubtedly improved since the late 1980s and early 1990s, developments in the progression of women to senior roles remain an issue.

It is widely reported that women dominate the UK publishing workforce, and this is borne out in data. In their 2020 UK Publishing Workforce report, the Publishers Association (PA) note that '[w]omen continue to dominate the workforce with females accounting for almost two thirds of respondents (64%) and half of executive leadership and senior management positions [are] held by women (52% and 55% respectively)' (Publishers Association, 2021, p. 6). There was a slight increase to these figures in the 2022 report, with women accounting for 66% of the publishing workforce and 56% and 60% of people in executive leadership and senior management positions, respectively (Publishers Association, 2022, p. 7). However, the drop off in the representation of women within the workforce (of up to 10%) between entry-level or lower/middle-management and senior leadership roles suggests that the kinds of gendered barriers to more senior and executive positions in the industry highlighted by Boyars in 1988 may remain. Additionally, the gender pay gap (as well as the ethnicity pay gap, which will be discussed later in this chapter) remains an issue for many publishers. In 2018, it was reported that many in the industry 'expressed frustration at the latest round of gender pay gap reports, which showed little progress had been made since 2017' (Chandler, 2018). On the publication of publisher reports in April 2018 (since 2017, all companies with 250 or more employees are legally required to report gender pay gap data (GOV.UK, 2023)), it was revealed that 'around half of firms where the pay gap already favoured men saw the margin widen even further' with any improvements being 'marginal' (Chandler, 2018). Some academic publishers had reported similarly poor improvements the year before with 'Taylor & Francis (T&F), Wiley, SAGE and Cambridge University Press . . . all showing gaps in favour of men, particularly in bonus payments, and all having women under-represented in the upper pay quartile' (Onwuemezi, 2018). More recently, publishers have reported progress in closing such gaps. Following the publication of 2022 Gender Pay Gap reports, a 'limited analysis' of 11 publishers by *The Bookseller* demonstrated that 'seven [publishers] have seen a decrease in the median hourly pay gap between the inaugural year of compulsory reporting in the UK, 2017/18, and 2021/22' (Brown, 2022). Reflecting on this data, Ruth Howells, the PA's deputy director of external affairs, noted that the

> reverberations of the [COVID-19] pandemic . . . are likely to impact reporting to some extent. . . . But overall things are moving in the right direction and data remains central to the industry's efforts around all aspects of diversity and inclusion.
>
> (Brown, 2022)

The overall point here being that the current issues faced by publishing and other Creative Industries, barriers to access and career progression, a lack of 'diversity' (both in terms of workforce and content development and creation), centralisation and concentration of the industry in specific areas of the country, pay gaps and systemic inequalities more broadly, are not new. Most importantly, knowledge of such issues—even if not necessarily identified as issues or problems and accepted as 'the way the industry works'—has been prevalent for decades. Publishing is not unique in this. The Creative Industries in general struggle with how to effectively respond to and 'manage' these issues as evidenced by the multitude of academic and industry research, surveys, and reports that identify such problems within specific sectors (see, e.g. on video games: Prescott and Bogg, 2011; Settle et al., 2013; UKIE, 2015; Harvey, 2019; and, Stang, 2023; on fashion: UK Fashion and Textile Association, 2020; and, Doyle and Moore, 2023; on craft: Spilsbury, 2018; Patel, 2020, 2021, 2022; on music: Bennett, 2018; Green, 2020; Das, 2022; UK Music, 2022[2]; Musician's Union, 2023; on film and television[3]: Randle et al., 2007; Directors UK, 2015; Eikhof et al., 2019; Newsinger and Eikhof, 2020; Nwonka and Malik, 2018; Nwonka, 2020; Creative Diversity Network, 2023) and across the Creative Industries more broadly (see, e.g.: Oakley, 2006; O'Brien et al., 2016; Alacovska and O'Brien, 2021; Brook et al., 2020; O' Brien and Arnold, 2022). As will be discussed presently, the Publishing industry and Publishing scholarship have also began reckoning with some of these key points. However, the industry has some catching up to do when it comes to active and critical discussions surrounding policy matters (both industry and cultural), particularly in relation to access, inclusion, and 'diversity'.

Problematising 'Diversity'

Before moving into a detailed discussion about the key trends and issues highlighted by existing Creative Industries literature and policy documents that also impact the Publishing industry, it is worthwhile taking some time to discuss and problematise some of the terms that have historically been favoured when discussing access, inclusion, and equity in the Creative Industries. It is notable that a lot of the existing policy reports and academic analyses pertaining to the Creative Industries workforce focus, either explicitly (including 'diversity' in publication titles) or implicitly (referring to data categorised by protected characteristics as a means of comparison to the assumed baseline/default of white, middle-class males), with the notion of 'diversity' but, it is important to take a moment to explore how the term 'diversity' is often utilised in such discourses and how it should be problematised.

Writing in 2006, Ahmed and Swan quote Benschop's (2001) examination of Human Resource Management (HRM), workplace diversity, and performance. Benschop notes how 'Authors with an interest in diversity have recently criticized HRM theories for representing "employees" as a generic category' (Benschop, 2001, p. 1166) (cited in (Ahmed and Swan, 2006, p. 96)). For Benschop, the emerging focus on 'diversity' in relation to equality and diversity policies and initiatives raised fundamental issues relating to the catch-all application of such terms:

> The challenge of diversity is much more than a change in terminology from categories like gender, ethnicity, age and class to the more encompassing and concealing term 'diversity'. In contrast to gender and other categories of identity, which are often represented as sources of social inequality in organisations, 'diversity' does not so powerfully appeal to our sense of social justice.
>
> (Benschop, 2001, p. 1166) (cited in (Ahmed and Swan, 2006, p. 96))

As Ahmed and Swan expand:

> The 'turn' to diversity has led to the term 'diversity' being used on its own or with the term 'equality', such that people increasingly talk about doing 'E & D' work. The politics of this turn has been much debated within critical race and post-colonial studies, feminist studies, as well as critical management studies. . . . This shift has meant that other kinds of vocabularies are no longer used, or at least are no longer central to policy debates, including terms such as 'equal opportunities', 'social justice', 'anti-racism' and 'multiculturalism'. These terms have complex histories, which are bound up with the history of different political movements, including the women's movement as well as the anti-racist movement. When the terms disappear from policy talk, a concern is that such histories might also disappear.
>
> (Ahmed and Swan, 2006, p. 96)

As Benschop, Ahmed, and Swan argue, the term 'diversity' is not only often used as an umbrella term to encompass protected characteristics or 'categories of identity' that are considered to be in the minority and therefore particularly vulnerable to discrimination and social injustice(s), but it has also come to be used as 'policy talk' that attempts to reference a range of distinct concepts and critical models. While many of these concepts, critical models, and categories of identity intersect,[4] attempting to capture their nuances and intersections under one label can dilute meaning and homogenise the categories or concepts such a term attempts to encapsulate.

Ahmed notes elsewhere that

> 'Diversity' can be used as an adjective, as a way of describing the organization, a quality, or an attribute of an organization. The language of diversity can also be used normatively, as an expression of the priorities, values, or commitments of an organization.
>
> (Ahmed, 2012, p. 52)

Expanding on this, through a study of the diversity policy initiatives of two public service broadcasters in the UK (the BBC and Channel 4), Malik has argued that following two initial 'phases' of diversity work and policy that focused on multiculturalism and cultural diversity, there has been a shift to the notion of *creative* diversity (Malik, 2013, p. 228). For Malik, because 'the term "creativity" signifies a postmulticulturalist, falsely postracial understanding . . . the particular nuance inscribed in "creative diversity" originates from an emergent postracial discursive politics (not from postracial times) and toward economic rationalism' (Malik, 2013, p. 228). While Malik's focus here is diversity in relation specifically to race and racism, and she is using broadcaster diversity initiatives as a formative base of analyses, these arguments are pertinent to understanding how diversity as a concept is utilised within the Creative Industries more broadly and particularly within Publishing. Malik's comment that the linguistic shift to favouring 'creative diversity' is indicative of a swing to 'economic rationalism' in relation to diversity discourse(s) is especially relevant when discussing policy and industry understandings and applications of 'diversity' within Publishing, as the industry appears to remain focused on the commercial imperatives for improved 'diversity'. Ramdarshan Bold has discussed this in relation to contemporary publishing in the UK, noting how,

> in recent years, the media, the creative industr[ies], and policy makers have shown an increased interest in the inequality, and the lack of 'diversity' (i.e. work by racially minoritised authors), in cultural production. . . . Various campaigns and initiatives to promote 'diverse' writing and industry professionals have followed. Brouillette argues that conglomeration of the book publishing industry has had a negative impact on the 'diversity' of content and, in the case of Brouillette's study, that postcolonial authors tend to get exploited by the industry in order to make their work more profitable. As publishers become increasingly focused on profit, they are likely to cater to existing and dominant market demands.
>
> (Ramdarshan Bold, 2019, pp. 46–47)

The economic rationalisation of the benefits of an increase in 'diverse' representation in books (specifically in Young Adult fiction, in the case of Ramdarshan Bold's work) is what underpins the motivations of many publishers which 'do diversity' (to borrow Ahmed and Swan's phrase). Accordingly, for Ramdarshan Bold, 'Publishing, under neoliberalism, has meant that although multiculturalism, or "diversity", is being promoted and encouraged, it is done in a superficial way' (Ramdarshan Bold, 2019, pp. 47–48).

This is the context within which the rest of this chapter (and book) sits. First, the imperfect and problematic nature of the term 'diversity' is acknowledged and considered. As this chapter will refer to industry policy documents and initiatives that have relied on such terminology, its use is inevitable. However, it is hoped that the aforementioned discussion demonstrates that this analysis does not use the term uncritically. Second, as discussed in previous chapters, the neoliberal, market-driven nature of the publishing industry should be considered an overarching framework for the proceeding discussion and analysis as, if the position and status of Publishing as a Creative Industry is to be critically examined, particularly in relation to systemic inequities and inadequacies, the sociopolitical and economic context of the Creative Industries in the UK is crucial groundwork. The rest of this chapter will therefore consider some of the key issues and trends currently impacting Publishing and interrogate industry policies and initiatives developed in response.

Who is 'in' Publishing?

In June 2014, the DCMS released the 'Creative Industries: Focus on Employment' report which provided employment data about the Creative Industries workforce based on 'region and Devolved Administration, level of qualification, gender and ethnicity' (DCMS, 2014, p. 8). As well as providing a complete overview of Creative Industries employment across the UK (which stood at 1.71 million jobs in 2013, an increase of 10.1% since 2011) (DCMS, 2014, p. 14)), the report compared the Creative Industries according to the aforementioned terms as well as providing a breakdown for each industry within the sector. While this report provides some of the earliest data we have pertaining to workforce 'diversity' within publishing, before discussing the data the report contains, it is worthwhile spending some time dissecting its methodology.

As O'Brien et al. explain, the report relies on a methodology grounded in Creative Skillset's notion of 'creative intensity' (O'Brien et al., 2016, p. 118) or the 'proportion of the workforce in *creative* occupations' which 'separates the Creative Industries from other industries' (DCMS, 2014, p. 10, emphasis added). In other words, the report attempts to capture information about those who are in 'occupations [that] are closely related to a specific vision of work in a post-industrial economy, whereby work is centred on making a living based on citizens' capacity as creative individuals' and the production of 'immaterial products associated with services and intellectual property' (O'Brien et al., 2016, p. 118). This methodology leads to an arguably convoluted means by which the data in 'Creative Industries: Focus on Employment' is reported, since the analysis is presented on the basis of whether the data refers to the Creative Economy (CE) (creative jobs outside the Creative Industries as well as all those employed in the Creative Industries), Creative Industries (a subset of the Creative Economy which includes people working in the Creative Industries, and this can include creative as well as administrative roles), and Creative Occupations (a subset of the Creative Economy which includes all working in creative occupations, irrespective of the industry that they work in) (DCMS, 2014, p. 10). This is potentially problematic for two reasons. First, as O'Brien et al. argue:

> As McRobbie (2015) has suggested, this is simultaneously a narrative that promotes an idea of the culture of work in the CCIs as one in which creativity is located as a central mechanism of *la carrière ouverte aux talents*. In other words, the 'creative' job is supposedly open to everyone. In British policy and practice discourses, where citizens are rarely described as anything other than innately creative (O'Brien, 2014), it is then a short step, within policy and practices discourses, to suggest that those who are able to make a living by capitalising on their creativity are simply reaping the just desserts of talent and skill.
>
> (O'Brien et al., 2016, p. 118)

While O'Brien et al. problematise this from their perspective of the false assumption that 'creative' work (however it is defined) is inherently democratising and 'meritocratic' due to perceptions of success being based on (maybe innate) talent and skill, applying such ideas and conceptualisations of creative work specifically to publishing reveals the second key issue with this approach. As previously discussed, the production of books is an industrial practice that depends on manufacturing infrastructures to enable dissemination of the creative act. This is not to say that this is unique to publishing, as such (music, film, and television are in a similar position in that they depend on the manufacture of hardware and developments in technologies to improve production quality and processes), but publishing is perhaps unique in that it is one of the Creative Industries that still depends on the mass production of a particular physical object.[5] While Intellectual Property may be the key 'immaterial product' associated with the 'creative' work of the industry, the final product *is* material, and as will be discussed in Chapter 3, understandings of the cultural and economic value of publishing are intertwined with this materiality. Such conceptual concerns aside, there is also the fact that the methodological approach of this report mixes the Creative Economy and Creative Industries in such a way as to effectively merge and conflate datasets. Due to this, and the fact that this book has already made the case for focusing on a Creative Industries framework and definitions, only the data referring to the Creative Industries (as opposed to the Creative Economy, which includes both those with 'creative occupations outside the creative industries' and 'those employed in the creative industries' (DCMS, 2014, p. 10)) will be used.

According to the 'Creative Industries: Focus on Employment' report, the publishing sector appeared to fare better in relation to gender and race and ethnicity than its Creative Industry peers. Women held 48.5% of the 198,000 publishing jobs in the Creative Industries in 2013. This is higher than advertising and marketing (43.8%); architecture (27.8%); films, TV, video, radio, and photography (37.5%); and IT, software, and computer services (19.4%), but lower than museums, galleries, and libraries (68.4%) and music and performing and visual arts (51.2%) (DCMS, 2014, p. 33). However, Schwarzer (2010) and Baldwin and Ackerson (2017) have both noted how, like publishing and other Creative Industries, museums and galleries also have issues regarding the representation of women in higher-level positions and boards. Schwarzer argues that although women represent a significant proportion of those working in museums and galleries in the US, men 'dominate museums in two critical areas: power and money' (Schwarzer, 2010, p. 17). According to Schwarzer:

> Men hold sway over boards of directors, major donor lists, and pay scales. They occupy 53 percent of executive director positions at small and mid-sized museums, and 75 percent of CEO seats at the nation's largest and best-funded institutions. And, although the gender pay gap is narrowing from previous decades, as of 2007 women museum professionals earned, on average, 78 cents to every dollar earned by men in similar positions.
>
> (Schwarzer, 2010, p. 17)

Relatedly, in their analysis of gender equity and museum boards of trustees, Baldwin and Ackerson suggest that while there may be a gender parity or at least an awareness of the need to meet gender balance and attempts to do so, 'museums so often fail to "see" women as critical to their success' (Baldwin and Ackerson, 2017, p. 73). This leads Baldwin and Ackerson to argue that:

> [T]he importance of gender equity and inclusivity at the board level and in staff leadership has a lot, *if not everything*, to do with the value message it

sends to museum employees and volunteers, as well as to visitors, program participants, and funders.

(emphasis in original, Baldwin and Ackerson, 2017, p. 73)

While both Schwarzer's and Baldwin and Ackerson's studies are focused on the US museums sector, in 2018, the Courtauld gallery in London noted that although '70% of art museum curators are women . . . museum leadership retains a boy's club reputation' and that '[n]one of the top three most visited art museums (The Louvre, The British Museum and The Metropolitan Museum of Art) have had a female director, and only four of the directors of the top twenty-five museums are women' (*Why does gender parity in the arts matter?*, no date) thus suggesting that this is an issue systemic within museums and galleries, as it is in publishing.

When it comes to employment across the Creative Industries by ethnicity (according to the DCMS 'Creative Industries: Focus on Employment' report), in 2011, 8.1% of those working in publishing identified as being Black, Asian, or from other minority ethnic backgrounds (DCMS, 2014, p. 38).[6] This put publishing in fifth place in terms of the proportion of jobs within the sector by ethnicity in comparison to the other seven Creative Industries accounted for in the report (there was no data available on ethnicity for craft). The percentage of people working in publishing who identified as Black, Asian, or from other minority ethnic backgrounds increased to 10.6% in 2013, bringing publishing into second place behind IT, software, and computer services (15.6%) and in line with the Creative Industries overall total in 2013 (10.6%) (DCMS, 2014, p. 38). For context, the 2011 Census revealed that 14% of the UK population across England and Wales were from Black, Asian, and minority ethnic backgrounds.[7] However, in London, where the Creative Industries are predominantly based, 40.2% of the population identified as belonging to 'minority ethnic groups' (Office for National Statistics, 2012).

While this DCMS report provides an overall insight into workforce diversity in publishing, on the whole, there is a relative scarcity of longitudinal workforce data specifically about, and produced by, the publishing industry in the UK. In March 2004, *The Bookseller* published 'In Full Colour: Cultural Diversity in Publishing Today', an industry survey conducted in conjunction with decibel, 'a one-year initiative of Arts Council England, promoting cultural diversity in the Arts' with the 'long-term aim of changing the arts landscape forever, moving the arts towards a place where it is more representation of the society we live in' (Clee, 2004, p. 3). The report's editor, Danuta Kean, noted that it was the first study of its kind to examine 'cultural diversity' within the publishing industry (Kean, 2005). Kean noted that a survey of over 500 people in the industry revealed 'a profession that is predominantly white and middle class, and sometimes complacent' and that 'black [*sic*] and Asian publishing professionals felt marginalised and excluded from the networks that ensure career success' (Kean, 2005). Of the 523 people surveyed for the report, 87% (456) were white, with 'Asian, Black, Chinese and other ethnic groups combine[d] to make up the remaining 13%' (Holman, 2004, p. 4). However, in a discussion of the data, one of the report's authors acknowledges that 'given that the majority of respondents—77%—are based in London, where minority ethnic communities make up almost 30% of the total populations, there is nothing for the industry to feel complacent about' (Holman, 2004, p. 4).[8]

For Kean, a 'shocking revelation' of the report, was:

> [T]he sense of isolation felt by many black [*sic*] and Asian people in the industry. Full-blown racism was rare, but common among minority ethnic workers were experiences of institutionalised racism, tokenism and insensitivity. More than one recalled being hauled into meetings with minority ethnic authors about books they would not be working on because the publisher wanted the author to know that it had black [*sic*] or Asian employees. Minority ethnic publishers also spoke of the lack of role models and the sense that they were carrying the flag for their entire race.
>
> (Kean, 2005)

The report led to the founding of the Diversity in Publishing Network (DipNet) by the then head of Marketing at Walkers Books, Alison Morrison, and Elise Dillsworth, editor at Virago. The purpose of DipNet was twofold: 'to support minority ethnic people already in the industry; and to attract a more diverse group of people into publishing than the white middle classes who currently dominate employment and recruitment' (Kean, 2005). Accordingly, it is clear that the lack of inclusion of people of colour within the publishing industry and the explicit and implicit racism and microaggressions that those within the industry experience have not only been known to be a systemic issue within the industry for decades, but that the intersections of race and ethnicity and socio-economic background and class were also identified at the time.

However, 'In Full Colour' also reveals the problematic and, perhaps, cynical way in which such information and 'revelations' were received at the time. The article immediately following Holman's summary and brief analysis of the survey data in the 'In Full Colour' report, entitled 'Diversity Pays Dividends', argues that there is a commercial imperative to improving 'diversity' within the publishing sector. Despite noting that '[g]reater emphasis than ever before is being placed on encouraging cultural diversity as desirable in its own right', Hilary Macaskill discusses the fact that in the 2003 'Top 100 Report', the Race for Opportunity chairman, Allan Leighton, argued that:

> Diversity is not about equal opportunities or compliance, it's about being more competitive, especially in a downturn. . . . Over 100 private and

> public sector participants tell us they invest in challenging ignorance and apathy because they've taken a closer look at their marketplace. Quite simply, communities equal customers and potential employees. If you rely on traditional perceptions of who these groups are, you limit your pool of talent and your target market.
>
> (Allan Leighton, cited in Macaskill, 2004, p. 7)

Relatedly, reflecting on the industry's response to the 'In Full Colour' report, Kean argued that the

> biggest shock of all was that the laissez-faire attitude towards diversity meant publishers were missing out on the disposable income of Britain's black [*sic*] and Asian communities, worth an estimated £32bn. It is a potential market that a £1.5bn industry cannot afford to ignore.
>
> (Kean, 2005)

Such comments demonstrate that conversations in the 2000s surrounding what Squires has since referred to as publishing's 'diversity deficit' (Squires, 2017) foregrounded the commercial case for making changes to the UK publishing industry. Saha has explored this within the media and creative industries more broadly, demonstrating how 'calls for greater diversity in the media—in both policy and academic accounts—are shaped by the normative principles of a liberal pluralist model of media . . . that it should mirror exactly the make-up of a nation' (Saha, 2018, p. 79). This principle of media 'mirroring' the population is, as Saha explains, 'rationalized in increasingly economic terms in neoliberal contexts' and has been 'reframed as a commercial imperative (rather than as an ethical/moral one), where particular demographic groups become "recognized" as market niches' (Saha, 2018, p. 79). This was an argument made by the crime author, and former accountant at Deloitte, Abir Mukherjee during the Publishers Association's Building Inclusivity in Publishing conference in 2017. As one account of the conference and Mukherjee's comments reported:

> Aside from our moral obligation to build teams that reflect our diverse population and to produce content that speaks to everyone, there's also a profound financial incentive. Essentially, by failing to produce diverse books, the publishing industry is missing out on valuable audiences. Author Abir Mukherjee used the British Asian community as an example. In the 2011 census, 5% of the British public described themselves as British Asians. The British Asian community are active library users, but a recent survey showed that approximately 50% had never been inside a bookshop. Another survey showed that 77% of British Asians felt that mainstream advertising had little or no relevance to them.
>
> (Headon, 2017)

This example illustrates how the language and discussions around the need for improving 'diverse' representation within publishing (both in terms of output and workforce—as Mukherjee also lamented the industry's reliance on unpaid internships and failure to invest in and support 'BAME writers' (uczcmsm, 2017)) are often positioned within the context of neoliberal, market-force focused terms and conditions.

Another point of note in Macaskill's article is the fact that she refers to surveys and initiatives within other Creative Industries (namely journalism and broadcasting) to highlight how 'diversity' has become a key area of development for companies, despite '[s]tatistics on diversity in the media [being] thin on the ground' (Macaskill, 2004, p. 7). Indeed, it would take another ten years before a more systematic approach was taken to collecting publishing industry workforce data following the 'In Full Colour' report (which, admittedly, was an extraordinarily small sample size of 523 people surveyed at a time when employment in the publishing industry in the UK was estimated to be around 200,000 (Department for Culture, Media and Sport, 2007, p. 8)). It was not until 2017 that the Publishers Association (PA) released their first ten-point action plan to 'tackle inclusivity and ensure that publishing better reflects the UK population' which included asking publishers to complete annual internal 'workforce audits' (Publishers Association, 2017).[9] This was accompanied by an initial survey of the industry by the PA which found that: 'women currently account for 49% of senior leadership roles but only made up 41% of executive board level. It also found that Black, Asian and minority ethnic (BAME) employees currently make up 13% of the publishing workforce' (Publishers Association, 2019). These figures instigated the PA to ask their members to agree to 'set industry-wide targets to seek to employ at least 50% of women in both senior leadership positions and executive level roles and ensure that 15% of employees are Black, Asian and ethnic minority people within the next five years', with targets reviewed annually based on improved data collection and annual industry workforce surveys (Publishers Association, 2019). The ten steps of the 2017 'Inclusivity action plan' asked publishers to:

1. Develop an inclusivity policy, which is embedded throughout the organisation and which has strong leadership commitment
2. Undertake an internal workforce audit and providing the PA with the data on an annual basis so that industry wide statistics can be published
3. Ensure all staff involved with hiring attend unconscious bias training
4. Nominate an inclusivity champion on your board or management committee who can monitor action on equality
5. Provide opportunities for flexible or agile working
6. Analyse job descriptions, recruitment strategies and interview practices for hidden biases
7. Develop a mentoring scheme that supports new staff or those at transitional career stages who are from traditionally underrepresented groups

8. Ensure there is a balanced speaker panel for any events you are running or speaking on
9. Consider hiring a Publishing Assistant apprentice or a Creative Access Intern
10. Become a publishing ambassador, as well as encouraging colleagues to give a careers talk to a local school or university

(Publishers Association, 2019)

The PA argued that the reason why they were focusing on improving the employment and promotion pipeline opportunities for women and people from Black, Asian, and minority ethnic backgrounds, as opposed to developing targets in what they referred to as 'other areas of inclusivity i.e. LGBT, Disability, Social Mobility', was because 'as an industry it was agreed to focus on two main areas in this initial stage' (Publishers Association, 2019).

This policy intervention from the PA is significant for a number of reasons. First, this action plan was the first to provide a clear set of guidelines, or targets, for publishing companies to work towards to prove their commitment to systemic change within their workforce and, also, the industry more broadly. While these kinds of interventions were widespread by this point across the Creative Industries and within specific sectors, particularly in the screen sector (see Eikhof et al., 2018 for a comprehensive review of workforce diversity research data about the UK screen sector), this was a relatively novel intervention in publishing. Since this intervention from the PA in 2017, they have published results of their 'diversity survey[s] of the publishing workforce' for 2018, 2019, 2020, 2021, and 2022. The year 2022 was the last year of annual reporting, as the PA has moved to biannual reporting and a 'new way of collecting data' for 2023–2026 (Publishers Association, 2022, p. 3). Table 2.1 consolidates the key workforce 'diversity' data from the PA reports from 2017–2022 (where available).

A first glance at the data in Table 2.1, which is arguably the most reliable workforce data we have about UK publishing, suggests that there have been minimal changes in some categories. For example, the overall percentage of women working in the industry has stayed somewhat stable within the circa 63–69% range. There seemed to be a dramatic change between the years of 2017, 2018, and 2019, with a dip in figures for 2018 (63.4%) compared to 2017 and 2019 (68.8% and 68.6%, respectively). The reports seem to indicate that the likely reason for this difference between consecutive years is the different survey (and question) response rates. The 2018 report notes that:

> [A]n accurate like for like comparison cannot be made between the 2017 and 2018 data, due to difference in response rates etc., the increase in data (+142.9%) obtained in 2018 suggests that these latest figures provide a

> truer reflection of the industry, with a slightly more equal gender balance (63.4% female and 36.1% male in 2018 vs 68.8% female and 30.8% male in 2017).
>
> (Publishers Association and Equal Approach, 2018, p. 9)

The 2019 report reiterates the similarities between 2017 and 2019 but does not speculate on what may have caused the 5% dip in 2018, despite claiming that the 2018 data was likely more accurate because of the higher response rates. The total responses to questions pertaining to gender balance in the workforce did increase exponentially year on year between 2017 and 2019. In 2019, 57 organisations took part in the PA's 'UK Publishing industry D&I Workforce Survey', this was up from 23 organisations in 2017 and 42 in 2018 (Publishers Association and Equal Approach, 2019, p. 28). The total responses across the 57 organisations in 2017, 2018, and 2019 were 2,648, 6,432, and 12,702, respectively (Publishers Association and Equal Approach, 2019, p. 28). Of the 57 organisations which contributed data in 2019, 9 submitted the existing data they had already collected, which accounted for 9,084 of responses, and 48 organisations shared the survey with their employees to collect responses, which accounted for 3,618 of the total (12,702) responses for the year (Publishers Association and Equal Approach, 2019, p. 28).

Further examination of the data reveals some of its potential pitfalls. With regards to how questions pertaining to gender and gender identity were navigated, for example in 2017, respondents who selected non-binary, other and prefer not to say were counted together, providing a total of 0.4% (Publishers Association and Equal Approach, 2019, p. 38). However, in 2018, the reported data provided the breakdown of these categories, showing that 0.1% of respondents identified as non-binary, 0.0% preferred another term, and 0.4% preferred not to say (Publishers Association and Equal Approach, 2018, p. 7). The 2018 and 2019 reports also provide separate questions for respondents who identify as transgender. The results for these questions arguably indicate how difficult capturing this kind of data is. For example of the 1,866 responses to the question 'Do you identify as transgender?' in 2018, 0.6% of respondents said yes, with 0.8% preferring another term, and 4.5% preferring not to say (Publishers Association and Equal Approach, 2018, p. 10). However, in response to the same question in 2019, of a total of 5,874 respondents, 0.2% responded yes, 0.4% said they preferred another term, and 1.9% said they preferred not to say (Publishers Association and Equal Approach, 2019, p. 39). What is interesting here is that despite there being a 214% increase in the number of responses between 2018 and 2019, the 2019 figures indicate that there were either fewer people working in publishing who identified as transgender (0.2% compared to 0.6% in 2018), preferred another term (0.6% in 2018 and 0.4% in 2019), or preferred not to say (4.5% in 2018 and 1.9% in

Table 2.1 Workforce Diversity Data from Publishers Association Workforce Diversity Reports 2017–2022

The Year Report Was Published	*Gender*			*Race and Ethnicity*	*Sexuality*	*Disability/Long-Term Health Conditions (LTHC)*		*Socio-economic Status*	*Level of Education*	
	Women in the Workforce	*Women in Senior Leadership*	*Women at Executive Board Level*	*Black, Asian, and Minority Ethnic*	*LGBT+*	*Disability/ LTHC*	*Mental Health*	*Socio-Economic Status (Respondents from Professional Backgrounds)*	*Privately Educated/ Attended Fee-Paying School*	*Educated to Degree Level*
2017	68.8%	49%	48%	13%	4.5%	2.3%				84.5%
2018	63.4%	56%	48%	11.6%	8.2%	5.4%	25.5%*		18.8%	83%
2019	68.6%	55%	53%	13%	10.3%	6.6%	40.20%	48.5%†	18.8%	83.8%
2020	64%	55%	52%	13%	11%	8%	46%	74%	19%	82%
2021	63%	56%	52%	15%	13%	13%	43%	67%	19%	83%
2022	66%	60%	56%	17%	15%	16%	49%	66%	17%	82%

* In the 2018 PA Workforce Diversity report, mental health was included as a sub-section in the question about disability and LTHCs, whereas from 2019 to 2022, it was treated as its own distinct question.

† In 2019, the question asked to ascertain the socio-economic status of respondents (based on whether their parents, guardians, or caregivers came from professional backgrounds) was 'How would you classify the primary job of your parent/s or carer/s throughout their career (Please select all that apply)?'. This was changed in the 2020 survey to: 'Which of the following best describes the type of work that the primary household earner undertook during your childhood?' Accordingly, while the 48.5% figure is not a like-for-like data point, it is the most relevant for the category in question.

2019) or there were fewer people willing to disclose this information via the survey (Publishers Association and Equal Approach, 2019, p. 40). If we apply the argument that the PA gave in the 2018 report regarding data being a 'truer reflection of the industry' if there are more respondents, the 2019 data regarding transgender employees appears to be yet another anomaly (Publishers Association and Equal Approach, 2018, p. 9). In the reports for 2020, 2021, and 2022, the presentation of the data was much simpler, with each report making the following, near identical, statement:

> Respondents were asked if their gender identity differed from the gender that they were assigned at birth. 0.6% of respondents said it differed with 98% saying that it remained the same. This corresponds with estimates by the Government Equalities Office that there are approximately 200,000 to 500,000 trans people in the UK, around 1% of the population.
>
> (Publishers Association, 2021, p. 16)

The 0.6% included here relates to the data gathered for the 2020 report; however, in 2021 and 2022, this rose to 1%, making the number of people working in publishing who identify as transgender align with the UK government's estimate at the time that circa 1% of the population identified as transgender. However, the UK census data published in 2021 revealed that:

> Around 262,000 people (0.5%) said their gender identity and sex registered at birth were different. Not all of those 262,000 people identified explicitly as transgender. Around 48,000 people (0.1%) gave their identity as 'trans man' and another 48,000 (0.1%) gave their identity as 'trans woman'. 118,000 (0.2%) did not provide a write-in response. A further 30,000 identified as non-binary and 18,000 wrote in a different gender identity.
>
> (UK Parliament, 2023)

It is important to examine this data in detail for two reasons. First, in recent years, the transgender population in the UK has been subject to particularly hostile attacks both by the UK government and within society more broadly. Hate crimes against transgender people hit a record high in the UK in the year ending March 2023 (Goodier, 2023), and political leaders have promulgated hostile, and at times false, rhetoric about the trans community in the UK (for more, see: Billson, 2023; Ferreira, 2022; Gross et al., 2023; and, Allegretti, 2023). This has also been an issue within the publishing industry. In order to highlight this, a group of people from the sector wrote an open letter in 2021 to the industry's leading trade magazine, *The Bookseller*, stating that 'transphobia is still perfectly acceptable in the British book industry' and that 'what is needed is "quiet statements of acceptance from companies and organisations within our industry"' (Wood, 2021).[10] Second, the complexity around this data demonstrates how potentially unreliable workforce demographic data can be as surveys cannot necessarily be entirely representative of specific minority groups as figures can be so small as to risk undermining anonymity. As Morrel-Samuels has noted: '[i]Including demographic questions, [in workforce surveys] can dramatically depress employee response rates, especially when respondents feel that their anonymity may be jeopardized' (Morrel-Samuels, 2002).

Table 2.1 also reveals that only the 2020–2022 reports included data relating to socio-economic background, level of education of the workforce, and mental health. This aligns with broader discussions within the publishing sector, and Creative Industries, about these factors becoming more prevalent in recent years. For instance the 'Panic! Social Class, Taste and Inequalities in the Creative Industries' report published in 2018 revealed that only 12.6% of people working in publishing were from working-class backgrounds (this was slightly higher than film and television at 12.4% but lower than music, performing, and visual arts at 18.2%) (Brook et al., 2018, p. 12). *The Bookseller* also conducted its own surveys into class and socio-economic background of those working in publishing in 2019 and 2022. The 2019 survey (of 1,167 people) found that '[a]lmost 80% of people in the publishing industry who see themselves as working class feel that their background has adversely affected their career' and that 'many respondents described feeling alien in the publishing trade, with their education and financial background meaning that they have struggled to secure internships, live in London, embrace the networking culture and progress through the industry' (Wood, 2019). The problem with this survey, however, was the fact that it required respondents to self-identify as being from working-class origins, and it is proven that many people misidentify themselves as working class (see Friedman et al., 2021; and Evans and Mellon, 2016, for more). Reflecting on *The Bookseller* 2019 class survey in 2022, the working-class author and founder of the Working Class Writers Festival, Natasha Carthew, noted how many of the social, economic, and cultural barriers that affected working-class people working in publishing in 2019 remained or had gotten worse following the COVID-19 pandemic (Carthew, 2022). While Carthew wrote from the perspective of writers, many of the barriers, or 'hindrances', to access to the industry including, 'a lack of time or space, lack of confidence, childcare costs, . . . no industry mates to give you a leg up, digital exclusion (lack of tech/phone minutes/a laptop for Zoom meetings), and a lack of role models from similar backgrounds' are also applicable to those from working-class backgrounds seeking work in publishing (Carthew, 2022).

To return to Table 2.1, the categories in which we see the largest increases in workforce identification over the years are mental health and disability/LTHC(s). Responses pertaining to mental health alone almost doubled over four years. Bearing in mind that the COVID-19 pandemic began during these four years, and it was widely recognised that this had a significant impact on many people's mental health across almost all demographics (WHO, 2022; Mind (no date); and University of Oxford, 2023), this increase in the number of people working in publishing indicating that they have ongoing problems with their mental health also aligned with a number of debates within the industry about its working culture. In a report published in May 2022, it was revealed that 69% of respondents working in publishing reported feeling burnout (defined by the World Health Organization as 'chronic workplace stress' (WHO, 2019) and 64% felt that their job had negatively impacted their mental health (Bayley, 2022). The survey prompted the author Anna Vaught to write a response to say that authors are also impacted, experiencing 'increasingly disappointing sales, events getting cancelled, rights not being sold in a sluggish and catching-up market, frayed tempers and increased ghosting from editors' (Vaught, 2022).

With regards to disability and LTHCs, there was a near 600% increase in respondents identifying as having a disability or LTHC between 2017 and 2022. However, far from being indicative of the industry hiring more people with a disability or an LTHC, this upturn may reflect a change in respondents' willingness to disclose this information or a change in how such data is gathered.[11] As Wilton has found, one of the main reasons why people may not disclose a disability or LTHC to their employer is a 'belief and/or previous experience that knowledge of impairment would substantially reduce the worker's chance of being hired or retaining an existing position' (Wilton, 2006, p. 35). Similarly, in their study of UK Film and TV, Randle and Hardy found that the production-based nature of work in film and TV 'which is characterized by short-term contracts, long, intensive working days and a high-speed labour process' (2017, p. 449) is 'creating and maintaining inequalities for people with impairments and other minorities more generally' (2017, p. 459). Mitchell has detailed how similar working cultures in publishing impact disabled workers or 'publishing hopefuls' in the 2021 report 'Access Denied: Disability, Employment and the UK Publishing Industry'. Reflecting on responses from an industry-wide survey and interviews with individuals working in publishing, Mitchell explains how

> [A] culture of stress and overworking, including fast-paced work environments, disproportionately impacts disabled people who might not be able to work at that level as consistently as non-disabled employees. According to survey respondents, in publishing this involves expectations to do work outside of contracted hours, including to socialise and network, read widely, and keep on top of trends in the industry. Mentions were also made of the popularity of evening events in the industry, where attendance was either required as part of the employee's job role or encouraged for networking. These were particularly difficult for disabled respondents to

> navigate due to fatigue, noise, a lack of accommodation for dietary requirements, sensory overload, or a general lack of accessibility.
>
> (Mitchell, 2021, p. 42)

Mitchell's report ends with a series of recommendations for the publishing industry to consider based on her findings, which range from employers improving how job advertisements are worded to calling for all internships and work placements to be paid (Mitchell, 2021, pp. 47–51).

Indeed, it is common for the kinds of industry reports discussed earlier to make explicit recommendations on improvements based on data and responses, or it is perhaps implicitly understood that such data can, and will, inform change. However, research has demonstrated the problem with this datafication of 'diversity' in the Creative Industries. As Newsinger and Eikhof have argued, the collection of data in and of itself does not 'transform the key industry practices and processes from which systemic disadvantage arises' and, if anything, can lead to 'counter productive implicit diversity policies and unintended consequences' (Newsinger and Eikhof, 2020, p. 57). Such unintended consequences can include time and money being invested in completing such data collection rather than investment in responding to (already well known and evidenced) inequities within industries. Or, as an interviewee noted in Ahmed's study of race equality and the politics of documents: 'You end up doing the document rather than doing the doing' (Ahmed, 2007, p. 599). Another issue is that such data is part of the work of using policies to 'rationali(se) in neoliberal terms . . . the benefits of diversity for competition and economic growth, rather than for political, let alone ethical or moral, reasons' (Saha, 2018, p. 78). In other words, quantifying 'diversity' reduces it to a focus on improving percentage points rather than embedding interventions.

As this chapter has shown, the UK publishing industry grapples with significant issues regarding access, inclusion, and representation among its workforce (as well as what it publishes). Such issues are not unique to publishing, with almost all other Creative Industries in the UK operating with the same problems. However, what is perhaps unique to publishing is the fact that it 'remains one of the worst [Creative Industries] sectors in terms of social mobility and structural inequalities' (Shaw, 2020). As one of the oldest creative industries, publishing has perhaps clung on to traditional notions of who should be involved in the creation of cultural products and how these should be presented to consumers. And, as the next chapter will explore, this traditionalistic approach to art and creative production has flourished within the neoliberal environment in which the Creative Industries have prospered in the UK.

Notes

1 Such assumptions of inherent progression and liberalisation in sociocultural and political thought and politics within the UK should not be taken

for granted, particularly in relation to government policy and aligning media rhetoric. Since coming to power in the 2010 general election, successive Conservative governments and Prime Ministers have ruled the UK with economically and socially conservative agendas and policies, with many news media outlets (particularly long-standing, 'traditional' media outlets such as broadsheet newspapers and public service broadcasters) perpetuating and supporting (or at the very least failing to interrogate) the austere measures taken by the government since 2010.

2 UK Music, an organisation that represents the 'collective voice of the UK's world-leading music industry', has been conducting their annual UK Music Diversity Survey since 2016 (*About*, no date).

3 The UK film and television sectors have arguably received the most critical attention regarding inequitable work practices and representation in content produced, so this is just a small snapshot of the kinds of publications that are available. For a more in-depth overview of the research knowledge base on the UK screen sector, see CAMEo, 2018.

4 For example critical race feminism (CRF) (Wing, 2003, 2014) and DisCrit (disability critical race studies) (Annamma et al., 2013).

5 Despite fears that e-books and e-reading devices would lead to the end of print books, particularly when Amazon announced that e-books outsold print books for the first time in 2011(Miller and Bosman, 2011), this prophecy has not played out as anticipated, with print sales leading in most markets by a significant margin (Fleck, 2024).

6 The 2014 DCMS report uses the acronym 'BAME' which stands for 'Black, Asian and minority ethnic'; however, this acronym and phrasing have been problematised as a term that homogenises a broad group of individuals 'who only shar[e] the characteristic of not having white skin', as former chairman of the Commission for Racial Equality, Trevor Phillips, argued in 2015 (Ford, 2015). This book will only use the term when making reference to policy documents and data that has used it and will favour the term 'people/persons/creators of colour' otherwise. A full discussion and dissection of the Creative Industries' use of the term 'BAME' can be found in Malik et al. (2022).

7 Discussions of Census data reveal the problem of the use of terms like 'ethnic minority' to represent people of colour, as there are also white ethnic minorities that are counted in Census data, as the UK government uses 'ethnic minorities to refer to all ethnic groups except the white British group . . . such as Gypsy, Roma and Irish Traveller groups' (GOV.UK, no date).

8 It is worth highlighting that this is a small sample size.

9 To compare this intervention to those from other CIs, Directors UK, Creative Skillset, and Equity had all published reports, guidelines, and industry plans to highlight and attempt to intervene on issues pertaining to inequity in the UK screen sector from 2014/2015 onwards.

10 Harry Potter author J.K. Rowling has been one of the most well-known and vocal authors to express anti-trans rhetoric on her social media platforms in recent years. For examinations of the harms of her rhetoric, see Gwenffrewi (2022) and Miller (2024).

11 No methodology for the PA Workforce Diversity report was provided. In 2018, the PA stated that the method of data gathering included asking publishers for their existing data. If there was no existing data, the diversity and inclusion consultancy, Equal Approach (EA), provided a survey that publishers could disseminate among employees. However, as the existing data and EA survey were both mediated by employers, it is possible that employees had not disclosed disabilities (and so would not be accounted for in the existing data) or did not wish to complete the EA survey in case this indirectly led to disclosure.

References

About. (no date) *UK Music*. Available at: https://www.ukmusic.org/about/ (Accessed: 17 September 2023).

Ahmed, S. (2007) '"You end up doing the document rather than doing the doing": Diversity, race equality and the politics of documentation', *Ethnic and Racial Studies*, 30(4), pp. 590–609. Available at: https://doi.org/10.1080/01419870701356015.

Ahmed, S. (2012) *On Being Included: Racism and Diversity in Institutional Life*. Durham: Duke University Press.

Ahmed, S. and Swan, E. (2006) 'Doing diversity', *Policy Futures in Education*, 4(2), pp. 96–100. Available at: https://doi.org/10.2304/pfie.2006.4.2.96.

Alacovska, A. and O'Brien, D. (2021) 'Genres and inequality in the creative industries', *European Journal of Cultural Studies*, 24(3), pp. 639–657. Available at: https://doi.org/10.1177/13675494211006095.

Allegretti, A. (2023) 'Prominent Tory ejected from conference after heckling home secretary', *The Guardian*, 3 October. Available at: https://www.theguardian.com/politics/2023/oct/03/prominent-tory-ejected-from-conference-after-heckling-home-secretary (Accessed: 6 October 2023).

Annamma, S.A., Connor, D. and Ferri, B. (2013) 'Dis/ability critical race studies (DisCrit): theorizing at the intersections of race and dis/ability', *Race Ethnicity and Education*, 16(1), pp. 1–31. Available at: https://doi.org/10.1080/13613324.2012.730511.

Baldwin, J.H. and Ackerson, A.W. (2017) *Women in the Museum: Lessons from the Workplace*. London: Routledge.

Bayley, S. (2022) 'Trade facing industry-wide burnout, Bookseller survey finds', *The Bookseller*. Available at: https://www.thebookseller.com/news/trade-facing-industry-wide-burnout-bookseller-survey-finds (Accessed: 16 May 2023).

Bennett, T. (2018) '"The whole feminist taking-your-clothes-off thing": Negotiating the critique of gender inequality in UK music industries', *IASPM Journal*, 8(1), pp. 24–41.

Benschop, Y. (2001) 'Pride, prejudice and performance: Relations between HRM, diversity and performance', *The International Journal of Human Resource Management*, 12(7), pp. 1166–1181. Available at: https://doi.org/10.1080/09585190110068377.

Billson, C. (2023) 'Rishi Sunak doubles down on anti-trans 'common sense' comments', *PinkNews | Latest Lesbian, Gay, Bi and Trans News | LGBTQ+*

News. Available at: https://www.thepinknews.com/2023/10/06/rishi-sunak-transphobic-comments-conservative-conference/ (Accessed: 6 October 2023).

Brook, O., O'Brien, D. and Taylor, M. (2018) *Panic! Social Class, Taste and Inequalities in the Creative Industries*. London: Arts Emergency.

Brook, O., O'Brien, D. and Taylor, M. (2020) *Culture Is Bad for You: Inequality in the Cultural and Creative Industries*. Manchester: Manchester University Press.

Brown, L. (2022) 'Gender pay gap progress in publishing slow but 'things moving in the right direction'', *The Bookseller*. Available at: https://www.thebookseller.com/news/gender-pay-gap-progress-in-publishing-slow-but-things-moving-in-the-right-direction (Accessed: 17 September 2023).

CAMEo. (2018) *Workforce Diversity in the UK Screen Sector: An Evidence Review*. Leicester. Available at: https://le.ac.uk/~/media/uol/docs/research-institutes/cameo/cameo_workforce_diversity_report_for_bfi_2018.pdf?la=en (Accessed: 17 September 2023).

Carthew, N. (2022) 'Bookseller's working-class survey, three years on', *The Bookseller*. Available at: https://www.thebookseller.com/spotlight/booksellers-working-class-survey-three-years-on (Accessed: 30 October 2024).

Chandler, M. (2018) 'Publishing figures express frustration at gender pay gap results', *The Bookseller*. Available at: https://www.thebookseller.com/news/publishing-figures-hit-out-shocking-gender-pay-gap-results-983491 (Accessed: 17 September 2023).

Clee, N. (2004) 'Diversity makes business sense', *In Full Colour: Cultural Diversity in Book Publishing Today*, 12 March, p. 3.

Creative Diversity Network. (2023) *Diamond: The Sixth Cut 2021–22*. London: Creative Diversity Network. Available at: https://creativediversitynetwork.com/wp-content/uploads/2023/07/Diamond-The-6th-Cut-July2023.pdf.

Das, S. (2022) *BE THE CHANGE: Measuring the Music Industry's Inclusivity and Diversity Issue*. MIDiA Research. Available at: https://www.midiaresearch.com/blog/be-the-change-measuring-the-music-industrys-inclusivity-and-diversity-issue (Accessed: 17 September 2023).

DCMS. (2007) *Creative Industries Economic Estimates Statistical Bulletin*. Department for Culture, Media and Sport. Available at: https://assets.publishing.service.gov.uk/government/uploads/system/uploads/attachment_data/file/78107/CreativeIndustriesEconomicEstimates2007.pdf (Accessed: 1 October 2023).

DCMS. (2014) *Creative Industries: Focus on Employment*. GOV.UK. Available at: https://www.gov.uk/government/statistics/creative-industries-focus-on-employment (Accessed: 20 September 2023).

Directors UK. (2015) *UK Television: Adjusting the Colour Balance: Black, Asian and Minority ethnic Directors in UK Television Production*. London. Available at: https://d3gujhbyl1boep.cloudfront.net/uploads%2F1447243539508-os03d6qe4pmsra4i-7c96b125575ce06ca956559154962a0a%2FDirectors+UK+-+UK+Television%2C+Adjusting+the+Colour+Balance.pdf (Accessed: 17 September 2023).

Doyle, S.A. and Moore, C.M. (2023) 'Diversity, inclusivity and equality in the fashion industry', In E. L. Ritch, C. Canning, and J. McColl (eds.)

Pioneering New Perspectives in the Fashion Industry: Disruption, Diversity and Sustainable Innovation. Emerald Publishing Limited, pp. 105–114. Available at: https://doi.org/10.1108/978-1-80382-345-420231009.

Eikhof, D.R. et al. (2018) *Workforce Diversity in the UK Screen Sector: Evidence Review*. Leicester: CAMEo, University of Leicester.

Eikhof, D.R. et al. (2019) 'And . . . action? Gender, knowledge and inequalities in the UK screen industries', *Gender, Work & Organization*, 26(6), pp. 840–859. Available at: https://doi.org/10.1111/gwao.12318.

Evans, G. and Mellon, J. (2016) 'Social class: Identity, awareness and political attitudes: Why are we still working class?', *British Social Attitudes*, 33. Available at: https://ora.ox.ac.uk/objects/uuid:4139d3ab-9aef-4840-b706-c5982c64d576 (Accessed: 30 October 2024).

Ferreira, L. (2022) 'Ignore Braverman's 'dangerous' anti-trans talk, schools told', *openDemocracy*. Available at: https://www.opendemocracy.net/en/5050/parents-and-teachers-fears-for-trans-kids-after-bravermans-evil-speech/ (Accessed: 6 October 2023).

Fleck, A. (2024) *Infographic: E-Books Still No Match for Printed Books*. Statista Daily Data. Available at: https://www.statista.com/chart/24709/e-book-and-printed-book-penetration (Accessed: 19 December 2024).

Ford, R. (2015) 'Ethnicity labels are divisive, says Phillips', 21 May. Available at: https://www.thetimes.co.uk/article/ethnicity-labels-are-divisive-says-phillips-qptswxk3l93 (Accessed: 24 September 2023).

Francis-Devine, B. and Ferguson, D. (2020) '50 years of the Equal Pay Act'. Available at: https://commonslibrary.parliament.uk/50-years-of-the-equal-pay-act/ (Accessed: 17 September 2023).

Friedman, S., O'Brien, D. and McDonald, I. (2021) 'Deflecting privilege: Class identity and the intergenerational self', *Sociology*, 55(4), pp. 716–733. Available at: https://doi.org/10.1177/0038038520982225.

Goodier, M. (2023) 'Hate crimes against transgender people hit record high in England and Wales', *The Guardian*, 5 October. Available at: https://www.theguardian.com/society/2023/oct/05/record-rise-hate-crimes-transgender-people-reported-england-and-wales (Accessed: 6 October 2023).

GOV.UK. (2023) *Gender Pay Gap Reporting: Guidance for Employers*. GOV.UK. Available at: https://www.gov.uk/government/publications/gender-pay-gap-reporting-guidance-for-employers (Accessed: 17 September 2023).

GOV.UK. (no date) *Writing About Ethnicity*. Available at: https://www.ethnicity-facts-figures.service.gov.uk/style-guide/writing-about-ethnicity (Accessed: 24 September 2023).

Green, L. (2020) *Gender Diversity in the UK Film Music Industry*. University of Nottingham. Available at: https://eprints.nottingham.ac.uk/id/eprint/60220.

Gross, A., Fisher, L. and Parker, G. (2023) 'Tory focus on trans and gender issues sparks unease within the party', *Financial Times*, 3 October. Available at: https://www.ft.com/content/0832548c-3750-4500-82c2-455e6f92faa7 (Accessed: 6 October 2023).

Gwenffrewi, G. (2022) 'J. K. Rowling and the echo chamber of secrets', *TSQ: Transgender Studies Quarterly*, 9(3), pp. 507–516. Available at: https://doi.org/10.1215/23289252–9836176.

Harvey, A. (2019) 'Becoming gamesworkers: Diversity, higher education, and the future of the game industry', *Television & New Media*, 20(8), pp. 756–766. Available at: https://doi.org/10.1177/1527476419851080.

Headon, A. (2017) *Building Inclusivity in Publishing Conference [event report] | BookMachine*. Available at: https://bookmachine.org/2017/11/14/building-inclusivity-publishing-conference-event-report/ (Accessed: 29 September 2023).

Holman, T. (2004) 'Room for improvement', *In Full Colour: Cultural Diversity in Book Publishing Today*, 12 March, pp. 4–6.

Kean, D. (2005) 'A year in diversity', *The Bookseller*. Available at: https://www.thebookseller.com/features/year-diversity (Accessed: 25 September 2023).

Macaskill, H. (2004) 'Diversity pays dividends', *In Full Colour: Cultural Diversity in Book Publishing Today*, 12 March.

Malik, S. (2013) '"Creative diversity": UK public service broadcasting after multiculturalism', *Popular Communication*, 11(3), pp. 227–241. Available at: https://doi.org/10.1080/15405702.2013.810081.

Malik, S. et al. (2022) *BAME: A Report on the Use of the Term and Responses to It: Terminology Review for the BBC and Creative Industries*. Birmingham: Sir Lenny Henry Centre for Media Diversity, University of Birmingham.

McRobbie, A. (2015). Be creative. Cambridge: Polity Press.

Miller, C.C. and Bosman, J. (2011) 'E-books outsell print books at Amazon', *The New York Times*, 20 May. Available at: https://www.nytimes.com/2011/05/20/technology/20amazon.html (Accessed: 19 December 2024).

Miller, L.J. (2024) 'J. K. Rowling's anti-trans rhetoric: Populist transantagonism', *Quarterly Journal of Speech*, 110(3), pp. 479–488. Available at: https://doi.org/10.1080/00335630.2024.2368562.

Mind. (no date) *The Impact of Coronavirus on Mental Health | Mind Research*. Available at: https://www.mind.org.uk/about-us/our-policy-work/coronavirus-research/ (Accessed: 30 October 2024).

Mitchell, C. (2021) *Access Denied: Disability, Employment and the UK Publishing Industry*.

Morrel-Samuels, P. (2002) 'Getting the truth into workplace surveys', *Harvard Business Review*, 1 February. Available at: https://hbr.org/2002/02/getting-the-truth-into-workplace-surveys (Accessed: 30 October 2024).

Musician's Union. (2023) *MU Equality Action Plan*. Available at: https://musiciansunion.org.uk/about-the-mu/equality-diversity-and-inclusion/equality-action-plan (Accessed: 17 September 2023).

Newsinger, J. and Eikhof, D.R. (2020) 'Explicit and implicit diversity policy in the UK film and television industries', *Journal of British Cinema and Television*, 17(1), pp. 47–69. Available at: https://doi.org/10.3366/jbctv.2020.0507.

Nwonka, C.J. (2020) 'The new babel: The language and practice of institutionalised diversity in the UK film industry', *Journal of British Cinema and Television*, 17(1), pp. 24–46. Available at: https://doi.org/10.3366/jbctv.2020.0506.

Nwonka, C.J. and Malik, S. (2018) 'Cultural discourses and practices of institutionalised diversity in the UK film sector: "Just get something black made"', *The Sociological Review*, 66(6), pp. 1111–1127. Available at: https://doi.org/10.1177/0038026118774183.

Oakley, K. (2006) 'Include us out—Economic development and social policy in the creative industries', *Cultural Trends*, 15(4), pp. 255–273. Available at: https://doi.org/10.1080/09548960600922335.

O' Brien, A. and Arnold, S. (2022) 'Creative industries' new entrants as equality, diversity and inclusion change agents?', *Cultural Trends*, 0(0), pp. 1–15. Available at: https://doi.org/10.1080/09548963.2022.2141100.

O'Brien, D. et al. (2016) 'Are the creative industries meritocratic? An analysis of the 2014 British labour force survey', *Cultural Trends*, 25(2), pp. 116–131. Available at: https://doi.org/10.1080/09548963.2016.1170943.

O'Brien, D. (2014). Cultural policy: Management, value and modernity in the creative industries. London: Routledge.

Office for National Statistics. (2012) *Ethnicity and National Identity in England and Wales—Office for National Statistics*. Available at: https://www.ons.gov.uk/peoplepopulationandcommunity/culturalidentity/ethnicity/articles/ethnicityandnationalidentityinenglandandwales/2012-12-11#tab-Measuring-ethnicity-and (Accessed: 25 September 2023).

Onwuemezi, N. (2018) 'Four more academic publishers reveal gender pay gaps', *The Bookseller*. Available at: https://www.thebookseller.com/news/tf-wiley-sage-and-cup-reveal-gender-pay-gap-data-759561 (Accessed: 17 September 2023).

Owen, P. (ed.). (1988) *Publishing—The Future: by Leading Publishers*. London: Peter Owen.

Patel, K. (2020) 'Diversity initiatives and addressing inequalities in craft', In S. Taylor and S. Luckman (eds.) *Pathways into Creative Working Lives*. Cham: Springer International Publishing (Creative Working Lives), pp. 175–191. Available at: https://doi.org/10.1007/978-3-030-38246-9_10.

Patel, K. (2021) *Making Changes in Craft*. Crafts Council. Available at: https://media.craftscouncil.org.uk/documents/Making_Changes_in_Craft_-_Craft_Expertise_Phase_One_Report_2021.pdf.

Patel, K. (2022) '"I want to be judged on my work, I don't want to be judged as a person": Inequality, expertise and cultural value in UK craft', *European Journal of Cultural Studies*, 25(6), pp. 1556–1571. Available at: https://doi.org/10.1177/13675494221136619.

Prescott, J. and Bogg, J. (2011) 'Segregation in a male-dominated industry: Women working in the computer games industry', *International Journal of Gender, Science and Technology*, 3(1). Available at: https://genderandset.open.ac.uk/index.php/genderandset/article/view/122 (Accessed: 17 September 2023).

Publishers Association. (2017) *Diversity Survey of the Publishing Workforce 2017*. Available at: https://www.publishers.org.uk/publications/diversity-survey-of-the-publishing-workforce-2017/ (Accessed: 20 September 2023).

Publishers Association. (2019) *PA Launches 10 Point Inclusivity Action Plan*. Available at: https://web.archive.org/web/20190305231338/

https://www.publishers.org.uk/news/releases/2017/pa-launches-10-point-inclusivity-action-plan/ (Accessed: 20 September 2023).

Publishers Association. (2021) *UK Publishing Workforce: Diversity, Inclusion and Belonging 2020*. London.

Publishers Association. (2022) *The UK Publishing Workforce: Diversity, Inclusion and Belonging in 2022*. London: Publishers Association.

Publishers Association and Equal Approach. (2018) *Publishing Industry Workforce Diversity and Inclusion Survey 2018*. London: Publishers Association.

Publishers Association and Equal Approach. (2019) *UK Publishing Industry Diversity & Inclusion Survey 2019*. London: Publishers Association.

Ramdarshan Bold, M. (2019) *Inclusive Young Adult Fiction: Authors of Colour in the United Kingdom*. Cham: Springer International Publishing.

Randle, K. and Hardy, K. (2017) 'Macho, mobile and resilient? How workers with impairments are doubly disabled in project-based film and television work', *Work, Employment and Society*, 31(3), pp. 447–464. Available at: https://doi.org/10.1177/0950017016643482.

Randle, K.R., Kurian, J. and Leung, W.F. (2007) 'Creating difference: Overcoming barriers to diversity in UK film and television employment'. Available at: http://uhra.herts.ac.uk/handle/2299/4575 (Accessed: 17 September 2023).

Saha, A. (2018) *Race and the Cultural Industries*. Newark: Polity Press.

Schwarzer, M. (2010) 'Women in the temple: Gender and leadership in museums', In A.K. Levin (ed.) *Gender, Sexuality and Museums: A Routledge Reader*. London: Routledge, pp. 16–27.

Settle, A., McGill, M.M. and Decker, A. (2013) 'Diversity in the game industry: Is outreach the solution?', In *Proceedings of the 14th Annual ACM SIGITE Conference on Information Technology Education*. New York, USA: Association for Computing Machinery (SIGITE '13), pp. 171–176. Available at: https://doi.org/10.1145/2512276.2512283.

Shaw, K. (2020) 'Common people: Breaking the class ceiling in UK publishing', *Creative Industries Journal*, 13(3), pp. 214–227. Available at: https://doi.org/10.1080/17510694.2019.1707521.

Spilsbury, M. (2018) *Who Makes? An Analysis of People Working in Craft Occupations*. Crafts Council.

Squires, C. (2017) 'Publishing's diversity deficit'. In *CAMEo Research Institute*. University of Leicester.

Stang, S. (2023) 'Diversity', In *The Routledge Companion to Video Game Studies*. 2nd edn. Routledge.

uczcmsm. (2017) 'Building inclusivity in publishing conference 2017', *UCL DIS Student Blog*. Available at: https://blogs.ucl.ac.uk/dis-studentblog/2017/11/15/building-inclusivity-in-publishing-conference-2017/ (Accessed: 29 September 2023).

UK Fashion & Textile Association. (2020) 'How can the UK fashion and textile industry encourage greater diversity?', *UKFT*. Available at: https://www.ukft.org/uk-fashion-and-textile-industry-diversity/ (Accessed: 17 September 2023).

UKIE. (2015) *Student Data Sheet: Players, Diversity and Education.* Available at: http://ukie.org.uk/sites/default/files/cms/docs/Diversity%20and%20players.pdf.

UK Music. (2022) *UK Music Diversity Report 2022.* London: UK Music. Available at: https://www.ukmusic.org/equality-diversity/uk-music-diversity-report-2022/ (Accessed: 17 September 2023).

UK Parliament. (2023) '2021 census: What do we know about the LGBT+ population?', *House of Commons Library* [Preprint]. Available at: https://commonslibrary.parliament.uk/2021-census-what-do-we-know-about-the-lgbt-population/ (Accessed: 6 October 2023).

University of Oxford. (2023) 'Young people's mental health deteriorated at greater rate during the pandemic—major new study'. Available at: https://www.ox.ac.uk/news/2023-09-21-young-people-s-mental-health-deteriorated-greater-rate-during-pandemic-major-new (Accessed: 30 October 2024).

Vaught, A. (2022) 'Under pressure: the authors' perspective', *The Bookseller*. Available at: https://www.thebookseller.com/comment/under-pressure-the-authors-perspective (Accessed: 16 May 2023).

WHO. (2019) 'Burn-out an 'occupational phenomenon': International classification of diseases'. Available at: https://www.who.int/news/item/28-05-2019-burn-out-an-occupational-phenomenon-international-classification-of-diseases (Accessed: 18 December 2024).

WHO. (2022) 'The impact of COVID-19 on mental health cannot be made light of'. Available at: https://www.who.int/news-room/feature-stories/detail/the-impact-of-covid-19-on-mental-health-cannot-be-made-light-of (Accessed: 30 October 2024).

Why does gender parity in the arts matter? (no date) *The Courtauld.* Available at: https://courtauld.ac.uk/whats-on/gender-parity-arts-matter/ (Accessed: 24 September 2023).

Wilton, R.D. (2006) 'Disability disclosure in the workplace', *Just Labour* [Preprint]. Available at: https://doi.org/10.25071/1705–1436.107.

Wing, A.K. (ed.). (2003) *Critical Race Feminism: A Reader*. 2nd edn. New York: New York University Press.

Wing, A.K. (2014) 'Critical race feminism', In J. Solomos and K. Murji (eds.) *Theories of Race and Ethnicity: Contemporary Debates and Perspectives*. Cambridge: Cambridge University Press, pp. 162–179. Available at: https://doi.org/10.1017/CBO9781139015431.014.

Wood, H. (2019) 'Survey reveals extent to which working class feel excluded from book trade', *The Bookseller*. Available at: https://www.thebookseller.com/news/survey-reveals-extent-which-working-class-feel-excluded-book-trade-960066 (Accessed: 6 November 2023).

Wood, H. (2021) 'Open letter says 'transphobia acceptable in British book industry', *The Bookseller*. Available at: https://www.thebookseller.com/news/open-letter-says-transphobia-acceptable-british-book-industry-1257896 (Accessed: 30 October 2024).

3 Publishing Hierarchies

Culture, Commerce, and Capitalism

The adjacency of private enterprise, art, and culture is an uncomfortable one for many and has been a topic of debate throughout late capitalism. Books, like many other forms of cultural production, are what Pierre Bourdieu calls symbolic goods and have a 'two-faced reality' as both 'a commodity and a symbolic object' (Bourdieu, 1993, p. 113). As Bourdieu notes, this created:

> [A]n apparent paradox, as the art market began to develop, writers and artists found themselves able to affirm the irreducibility of the work of art to the status of a simple article of merchandise and, at the same time, the singularity of the intellectual and artistic condition.
>
> (Bourdieu, 1993, pp. 113–114)

Publishing encapsulates this dichotomous 'commodity versus symbolic good' condition. The antagonism of the duality between commercial enterprise and cultural aspiration in contemporary publishing is perhaps most evident when issues pertaining to the industry's employment and creative remuneration practices are examined. Concerns regarding publishing's working practices, salary thresholds, and inclusivity (both in terms of access into the industry and the diversity of who and what is published), are at a continuous simmer, cyclically boiling over into active discourse on social media and industry journals, before seemingly settling, often unresolved.

As discussed in Chapter 2, barriers to access and entry for creators (i.e. authors) and producers (i.e. the various in-house or outsourced roles required to publish books) are an issue across most Creative Industries and are not unique to publishing, but they are arguably exacerbated by two features of the culture of publishing which will be discussed in this chapter. The first is the notion that those who work in publishing do it for the love of the job, which not only ties into the idea that aspects of the process of publishing are instinctual to certain individuals (and therefore exclusive) but also leads to a perpetuation of poor working conditions as people working in the industry know it is hard to get in and feel lucky when they do. This issue of creative work as 'passionate work' (McRobbie, 2016, p. 89) is not unique to publishing, and

DOI: 10.4324/9781003187905-4

several scholars have examined it in relation to other creative industries (see, e.g. Banks, 2007; McRobbie, 2016; Bennett, 2018; Creus et al., 2020), but there is little critical discourse about it specifically in relation to publishing. The second feature relating to the culture of publishing, which is unique to the industry, is the notion that publishing is a superior form of cultural production compared to other creative enterprises. Perhaps more than any other creative work, there is a reluctance to reduce the process of writing, editing, and publishing a book to the sum of its parts. This is evidenced by the rhetoric surrounding the work of publishing, as well as how the most explicitly commercial facets of the industry—book selling and book consumption—are discussed and represented. As a result, long-standing tensions between art for its own sake and art as commercial imperative remain deep rooted in publishing.

For the Love of Books

In the first chapter of their 2008 book *How to Get a Job in Publishing: A Really Practical Guide to Careers in Books and Magazines,* Baverstock et al. open with a quote from the then Managing Director of Penguin Books, Helen Fraser, who said: 'It took me a long time to get my first job in publishing, but someone (a publisher) said to me, 'Everyone who really wants to get in does, so just persist', which I did—and it worked' (Fraser quoted in Baverstock et al., 2008, p. 3). Baverstock et al. follow this with a direct address to the reader, stating:

> Since you're reading this, chances are you are seriously considering a career in publishing. Tell someone that this is your ambition and they're likely to tell you, 'But of course it's practically impossible to get into publishing, you know'. Whether or not this is true . . . a lot of people give up before they even try. This book assumes a more robust attitude on your part: that you want to find out how the industry works, and what kind of people thrive within it.
>
> (Baverstock et al., 2008, p. 3)

The meritocratic neoliberalism of these statements (which will be unpacked momentarily) was toned down slightly for the second edition of the book, published in 2023:

> When you first tell people you want to work in publishing, magazines or the booktrade, you're virtually guaranteed to hear this: *get real. It's practically impossible to get into, and you've got no chance*. Or perhaps, more politely, *Oh! Um. Good luck*. . . . Are they right? Well, yes, jobs in publishing are highly sought after. . . . Despite this avalanche of negativity, we maintain if you really, really want to, you can make it, and that it's worth the effort to find a place with the world of publishing.
>
> (Baverstock et al., 2023, p. 1)

Given that this book was marketed as a title that will provide the reader with the knowledge and acumen they will need to pursue a career in publishing (and is a popular set text on university publishing courses in the UK), it is an interesting gambit to open with the frank restatement that publishing is a notoriously difficult industry to get into. And while the second edition of the book carried the caveat that '[b]uying this book doesn't guarantee you a job in publishing' (Baverstock et al., 2023, p. 6), the overall rhetoric provides an insight into how the industry is framed by those who are actively trying to help people pursue a career in publishing. Although the notion that 'everyone who really wants to get in does' was removed from the 2023 edition of the book, the reiteration that if you 'really, really want to, you can make it [in publishing]' endorses the view that work in publishing, and in turn the Creative Industries more generally, will come to those who want it, work for it, and, most importantly, deserve it. In other words, the industry works in a meritocratic and fair way.

In *Against Meritocracy*, Littler notes that 'Meritocracy today entails the idea that whatever your social position at birth, society ought to offer enough opportunity and mobility for 'talent' to combine with 'effort' in order to 'rise to the top'' (Littler, 2017, p. 1). Littler continues, arguing that:

> Meritocracy has long historical roots, but it also has a new face. It proclaims greater equality of opportunity for more people than ever before. We have been encouraged to believe that if we try hard enough we can make it: that race or class or gender are not, on a fundamental level, significant barriers to success. To release our inner talent, we need to work hard and market ourselves in the right way to achieve success.
>
> (Littler, 2017, p. 2)

However, as Littler expounds, this understanding of meritocracy is fundamentally flawed. For Littler, there are five key problems with the concept, all of which are relevant to this discussion of contemporary publishing. First, meritocracy only works if there is a system of hierarchy in which some people are more successful than others, in other words, '[n]ot everyone can "rise"' (Littler, 2017, p. 3). Second, the 'logic of meritocracy frequently (though not always) assumes that talent and intelligence are innate: it depends on an essentialised conception of intellect and aptitude' (Littler, 2017, p. 4). This is a particularly pertinent conceit in publishing which arguably retains the specious image of the lone creative worker, whether that be an editor red-penning manuscripts at their desk or an author sitting alone frantically typing. Third, contemporary understandings of meritocracy fail to recognise that achieving success is more difficult for some than others (Littler, 2017, p. 5). The fourth issue, which relates to the first, is the fact that meritocracy supports a tiered organisation of 'professions and status', again reinforcing a bottom versus top, or have versus have not, condition (Littler, 2017, p. 6). Finally, in endorsing and maintaining such systems of hierarchy, meritocracy 'functions as an ideological myth to obscure and extend economic and social inequalities' (Littler, 2017, p. 7). Indeed, as Chapter 2 demonstrated, it cannot be the case that publishing works in the meritocratic way that Fraser and the authors of *How to Get a Job in Publishing* suggest, because the existing inequities in the representation in the workforce (and what is published) do not support this argument. Fraser's personal example is further undermined when we consider the fact that her father was the prolific poet and literary critic George Saunders Fraser. While we cannot assume this would assure Helen Fraser a job in publishing, it does imply there would have been a social and cultural capital and experience she was privy to that not all those seeking a job in the industry could claim.

The assumption of meritocracy in publishing is so embedded that it has trickled down to those who do not yet hold a much sought-after position within the publishing work hierarchy. Alongside 'how to' guides, the internet is awash with advice on how to get into the industry from those who are still seeking employment or have just succeeded in acquiring their first role. There is a 'Publishing Hopefuls' Facebook group with 6.5k members (as of December 2024); the Society for Young Publishers, 'a volunteer-run organisation supporting junior and aspiring publishing professionals across the UK and Ireland' (SYP, no date); and volunteer-run online publications like *The Publishing Post*, a fortnightly magazine 'for those who wish to learn more about publishing, by providing a platform where, as contributors and readers, publishing hopefuls can develop industry-specific knowledge and skills, whilst showcasing their passion and love for the publishing industry' (*The Publishing Post*, no date). Advice to so-called 'publishing hopefuls' often include completing postgraduate degrees in publishing, seeking out (often unpaid) internships or work placements, and networking (in-person and online).[1] All of which have their own economic, social, and cultural barriers to access. Postgraduate education, for example, is expensive, with the average cost for a one-year Master's degree in the UK being over £8,000 for home students and between £17,000 and £18,000 for international students (Find a Masters, no date). This does not take into consideration living and accommodation costs if a student is living away from home (whether internationally or domestically). Similarly, low or unpaid internships require an individual to have another source of income to support completing work for no pay. The financial impact of this can be heightened by the fact that London, one of the most expensive cities in the world to work and live in, is the hub of publishing in the UK. This issue is so significant that the industry has recognised it and taken steps to respond. In 2017, Hachette partnered with The Book Trade Charity (BTBS) to 'offer subsidised accommodation in London to people starting out on careers in publishing. . . . The offer is geared towards to helping those for whom living in the capital is "prohibitively expensive"' (Cowdrey, 2017). The scheme was initially open to 'successful applicants for

[Hachette's] BAME [Black, Asian, and Minority Ethnic] trainee programme' and 'others starting out on their careers "on a needs basis"' (Cowdrey, 2017). This arrangement was treated as a pilot, with BTBS announcing in 2021 that they had completed an 'affordable housing development' which would see flats and bedsits rented to those starting their careers in the publishing industry for '40% cheaper than equivalent accommodation in the area' (The Bookseller, 2021). Furthermore, the UK cost-of-living crisis (Houston, 2022) is having an impact on people pursuing work in the Creative Industries more broadly, with 82% of people not applying for jobs in the sector 'because of financial barriers', which was 'an increase of 5% since 2021' (Majdan, 2023). And in June 2022, the author and Assistant Editor at Penguin Random House, Kasim Ali, questioned whether it was time for 'publishing to strike' due to the UK's current economic climate and the cost-of-living crisis 'outpacing meagre and hard-won wages' (Ali, 2022).

It is worthwhile focusing on the issue of low and/or unpaid internships in the Creative Industries here, given that it has been a focus in academic and industry discourse for a number of years (see Siebert and Wilson, 2013;Shade and Jacobson, 2015; Campbell, 2020; and Brook et al., 2020 for more). Writing in 2010, Hesmondhalgh highlighted the inherent tension with free and low-paid creative work/labour, arguing that '[m]any cultural industries now seem to their workers to be more competitive than ever, and staying ahead requires long hours and an intense relationship to the work' (Hesmondhalgh, 2010). While Hesmondhalgh recognises that such expectations of commitment and intensity are problematic and that some have argued that the structures of creative work empower 'control mechanisms that serve to discipline or seduce workers into putting a great deal of themselves into what they do, and tolerating precariousness and insecurity', he also recognises that the 'cultural industries provide significant opportunities for good work' (i.e. work that can be autonomous, creative, and fulfilling) (Hesmondhalgh, 2010). More recently, Brook et al. have argued that levels of, and tolerance for, the precariousness of unpaid work in the creative industries are stratified by 'age and career stage, and by social class origin' and that there are 'important differences [in experience] between those older, more established, cultural workers and those, often younger, who are more recent entrants to cultural careers' (Brook et al., 2020). Significantly, despite Brook et al. quoting an interviewee who stated that they were told they would not get a job in publishing without completion of an unpaid internship, their overall findings indicate that those working in publishing (as well as museums and galleries, and advertising and marketing) were 'less likely to have worked for free' (Brook et al., 2020b, p. 581).

However, we know that the kinds of social and cultural barriers Brooks et al. highlight are experienced by those working in publishing. In a 2024 report, Creative Access found that 73% of 392 people working in the Creative Industries surveyed believed there was 'class-based discrimination' in the Creative Industries (Creative Access, 2024, p. 4). The report notes that 'Class barriers [are] particularly pronounced in publishing', with 72% of people working in the sector believing class to be an issue within the industry (Creative Access, 2024, p. 8). Additionally, the report states that: 'While all sectors acknowledged working class representation as an issue, publishing stood out with 81% of respondents, nearly 20% above the average [across all CIs] (64%)' (Creative Access, 2024, p. 5). These figures align with the 2018 'Panic!' report (discussed in Chapter 2), which stated that the representation of people from working-class backgrounds in publishing was 'especially grave' with 'over a third of the workers from the upper middle class social origins and only about an eighth from working class origins' (Brook et al., 2018, p. 13).

Despite such issues and obstacles to access, like other Creative Industries, publishing is not only perceived as being a particularly desirable industry to work in but is also the one which is typically discussed in hyperbolic terms that reinforce notions of creative work as something which an individual pursues because of, to borrow *The Publishing Post*'s words, their 'passion and love' for the work. Such discourse evidences what Conor, Gill, and Taylor have identified as 'a powerful stereotype [that] has taken root and flourished' in relation to work in the creative industries (Conor et al., 2015, p. 2). This stereotype

> sees the typical 'creative' as driven by passion to Do What You Love (DWYL), prepared to work for long hours for little or even no pay, and requiring minimal support. It is significant to note the potency and pervasiveness of this personalized figuration of the 'creative' and how profoundly it has displaced important questions about working conditions and practices within the CCI, let alone issues of equality, diversity and social justice.
>
> (Conor et al., 2015, p. 2)

This 'do what you love' attitude is by no means a new measurement of Publishing work. Writing in 1988, the publisher and Chief Executive of Associated Book Publishers, a trade group for a number of imprints, Michael Turner, commented:

> [T]o the world outside, publishing has a somewhat romantic air. Public perception of what we actually do is often far from the mundane reality. To some extent we who work in the business perpetuate such myths for our own self-satisfaction.
>
> (1988, p. 12)

Turner continued, suggesting that:

> The stereotype publishing house must be a sort of rose-tinted Faber & Faber, where young graduates and middle-aged literati work in a nice

> Georgian residence in Bedford Square [London], rubbing shoulders with the likes of Craig Raine, Jeffery Archer and Graham Greene, where the pay is nothing much but the job satisfaction immense, where creativity is paramount and authors are lunched at the Garrick or the Groucho, depending on the age and trendiness of the host.
>
> (1988, p. 13)

Turner's tongue-in-cheek appraisal of the stereotypical aura surrounding publishing identifies some of the misplaced and romanticised assumptions about the sector and how it works, such as how pay may be low but job satisfaction makes up for this, but in the conclusion of this piece, in which Turner reflects on how publishing has changed in the 1980s and might change in the coming years, he also says:

> The large publishing group is a reality that is going to be an inescapable feature of the book world of the 1990s. Perhaps it will mean, slowly and perhaps bloodily, the end of some aspects of publishing as we know it and love it. . . . However, I have too much faith in the inextinguishable power of the writer and the ingenuity and enthusiasm of the publisher not to believe that they will both continue to flourish, and make the best use of the corporate environment.
>
> (Turner, 1988, p. 21)

Turner here alludes to the increasing conglomeration of publishing that had come to define the economic and business practice of the industry since the 1960s, accurately predicting that 'large publishing groups' were going to become the norm in publishing and potentially bring some of the more exceptional, and perhaps quixotic, elements of the industry to an end. However, rather than be dismayed by this, Turner is optimistic that people in publishing—writers and publishers—are so creative and dedicated to the cause that they will flourish in this potentially harsher and more ruthless 'corporate environment' (Turner, 1988, p. 21). The point Turner seems to make here is that 'publishing people' are uniquely positioned to avoid the corruption to creativity that big business threatens and also innovative enough to exploit the benefits of conglomeration. This is both a reiteration of the inherent passion and creativity of the publishing worker and a hint towards the incoming neoliberalism of business and culture that would define the UK Creative Industries in the 1990s.

More recently, Claire Squires' research examining the role of commissioning editors further highlights the romanticisation of publishing work. Squires interviewed a number of UK-based commissioning editors from a variety of publishers in 2016 and notes that the participants were all white, mostly female, and 'largely middle class' (with most self-declaring as such) (Squires, 2017, p. 28). This demographic spread is perhaps important, given what we know about the make-up of the publishing industry and Squires' findings. When asked how their individual tastes and preferences aligned with their company's strategies when reading manuscripts to acquire, the editors Squires spoke to responded using 'terms such as "instinct" and "gut reaction"' (Squires, 2017, p. 29). Several of the interviewees commented on the instinctual feeling and response they had to books, with one stating: 'it's more a kind of emotional feeling, or something in the pit of your stomach . . . it's all quite an unconscious thing to be honest . . . instinctive, . . . or feeling that something is right', and another: 'You almost learn to trust how your body is reacting to something because those books that you got super excited about are then going to be a hit, and then you think, "I've got that feeling again"' (Squires, 2017, p. 29). Such interpretations of how the role of being an editor, and therefore being the gatekeeper, tasked with selecting books for a publisher's list that will sell, not only potentially feed into the notions of roles within publishing being meritocratic—you either have that *feeling* or you do not—but also make the work of the editor literally undetachable from the individual. However, Squires notes that, despite such impassioned claims of the physiological responses to books from the interviewees, ultimately 'editors needed to fit their editorial taste-making and selection to their company environment' and '[g]ut reactions were, in actuality, learned business decisions, in constant negotiation with that environment' (Squires, 2017, p. 31). Elsewhere, Squires has argued that accounts of the 'sensory ways in which editors narrate their experiences of commissioning, both as a lived, felt experience, but also as part of a professional discourse . . . have self-mythologizing as well as mystifying tendencies' and that this correlates with 'the seeming need to occlude or render invisible aspects of professionalized reading and evaluation practices' (Squires, 2020b, p. 253). Such 'self-mythologizing' arguably contributes to the perpetuation of the romanticised view of publishing work that inspires aspiration to work in the industry: who does not want to read books they love for a living? But the perpetuation of publishing work and, in this case, editorial, as being a 'labour of love' (Eichhorn and Milne, 2016, p. 189) can also undermine the value of such creative work.

Creative work is here being understood in terms of Banks and Hesmondhalgh's definition as work that is 'geared to the production of original or distinctive commodities that are *primarily* aesthetic and/or symbolic-expressive, rather than utilitarian and functional' (emphasis in original, Banks and Hesmondhalgh, 2009, p. 416). This book has focused on what might be referred to as the 'behind the scenes' work of publishing; the workforce who, working with authors, take books from concept to publication. For the most part, the publishing workers are not the originators of the 'commodities' they are dealing with, but they play a vital role in bringing such 'aesthetic and/or symbolic-expressive' work to market. Using this definition for publishing work is not unproblematic. While recognising the problem of neoliberal economisation of cultural and creative industries, and therefore the commercialisation of creative endeavours, publishing is ultimately the business of creating a 'utilitarian and functional' product: the book. And it is the book that needs to sell in order to sustain the industry. This tension between culture and business is, as Banks has illustrated, central to the work of the creative worker:

> The creative cultural worker exists at the very axis point of political struggle between the forces of art and commerce. It is the creative worker, as the particular focus and embodiment of the art–commerce relation, who must most evidently balance the desire to indulge in disinterested, creative self-expression against the necessity of accumulation.
>
> (Banks, 2007, pp. 8–9)

This 'axis point' is evident, as Squires' work has highlighted, in the role of the commissioning editor, who is tasked with finding work they 'love' and which not only aligns with the publishing house's ethos and list but that is also economically viable for the publisher to invest in.

The other key aspect of publishing that is entrenched in the 'art versus commerce' tension is bookselling (and book buying), which, as will be discussed in the next section, is often embroiled in existential debates of value and need which not only obfuscate the commercial enterprise of bookselling but also perpetuate the hierarchising of the book as cultural product.[2]

Books Are Best

In addition to the record-breaking revenue generated by the publishing industry in 2022, in January 2023, it was announced that 'Indie bookshop numbers hit 10-year high in 2022' (Wood, 2023). This followed what appeared to be a resurgence in attention and regard for independent bookshops, reignited during the UK's national lockdowns which forced many independent bookshops to rethink how they could provide services to their local communities and consumers. Upon the announcement of the first national lockdown in March 2020, a number of independent bookshops shifted their focus away from instore sales to online and local delivery. Some bookshops, like Book Hive in Norwich, provided free postage for customers who ordered books on their website (Chandler, 2020), and the publisher Bloomsbury offered to support independent bookshops by 'invit[ing] bookshops to share its website and delivery channels' and giving '15% of the purchase price [of the book] back to the shop' (Comerford, 2020). Other booksellers made deliveries by hand, bike, and skateboard to customers who were self-isolating (Flood, 2020a). Such pivots were arguably key to independent bookshops, which tend to rely on hand-to-hand sales, footfall, and relationships within their local communities, due to the competition of online sellers like Amazon and supermarket chains, both of which can offer book-buyers significant discounts.

Indeed, reading was perceived to be one of the pastimes that people relied upon during national lockdowns. A report by The Reading Agency in April 2020 stated that 31% of people were 'reading more during lockdown' and that there was a 'particular spike among young people (18–24) where almost half (45%) are reading more than before lockdown' (The Reading Agency, 2020). These figures were echoed, and surpassed, in a survey by Nielsen Book who found that 41% of people (based on a representative sample of 1,000 people) stated they were reading more during lockdowns in early 2020 (Flood, 2020c). The data also suggested that people were spending more time reading. The average number of hours of reading per week increasing from 3.5 hours to 6 and '[m]ore than half (52%) of the respondents said they were reading more because they had more spare time, 51% said it was because they wanted to stay entertained, and 35% felt books were providing "an escape from the crisis"'(Flood, 2020c).

Access to books and reading was considered to be so imperative to the nation's health and well-being that some trade bodies called for books to be considered 'essential' items which would enable bookshops to stay open during national lockdowns.[3] In November 2020, the Booksellers Association (BA) wrote to the UK government to request they 'classify bookshops as essential retailers during England's second lockdown, as other retailers that sell books like WH Smith and supermarkets get to remain open' (Flood, 2020b). The arguments behind this were both commercial and ideological. In their plea to the government, the BA's managing director, Meryl Halls, called bookshops 'lanterns of civilisation' and 'beacons of hope', as well as arguing that bookshops remaining closed while other retailers who sold books (as well as other items) staying open was 'potentially ruinous commercially and . . . morally problematic' (Flood, 2020b). The managing director of Waterstones, James Daunt, also said that: 'It's not really very helpful when we [bookshops] all go bust and the big guys are going to be OK. It's ridiculous, and it's a tragedy' (Flood, 2020b). Squires commented on the irony of this protest, noting how:

> In 2020, books may be claimed as 'essential goods', but in previous decades, the argument was made—including in a Restrictive Practices Court case over the Net Book Agreement (NBA) in 1962—that books were 'different' to the mass of consumer products (Stevenson, 2019). For much of the twentieth century, the NBA regulated fixed prices for books, prevented discounting, and sustaining small bookshops. As Allen Lane, founder of Penguin Books stated in interview a few years after the NBA Restrictive Practices Court case, 'A book is not a tin of beans'.
>
> (Squires, 2020a, p. 3)

The point here being that books have been, and continue to be, treated as possessing the somewhat contradictory qualities of being both, as Squires puts it, 'essential *and* exceptional' (Squires, 2020a, p. 4). Norrick-Rühl and Koegler have also reflected on this notion of books being different to other forms of cultural production:

> [B]oth books and literature continue to be assigned an exceptional status—a status that is fundamentally rooted in the notion of an essential *difference* of books from other market goods. This includes the legal framing, given that the 'essential difference' of books has long been translated into hands-on legal regulations, whether active or passive, such as fixed book pricing or reduced VAT rates, which persist to date in many countries.
>
> (Koegler and Norrick-Rühl, 2023, p. 7)

In their study, Koegler and Norrick-Rühl argue that 'books and book culture might need to be *diverse* in order to legitimately count as *different*', earning 'protection and surplus income that strengthens publishers' and authors' structural positions via a diversification of voices both published and in gatekeeping positions' (emphasis in original, Koegler and Norrick-Rühl, 2023, p. 8). And while Koegler and Norrick-Rühl focus their discussion of the book as 'different' via the industry's need to diversify and the impact of digital developments, their premise that 'books might not need to be noneconomic or even anti-economic goods to prove themselves as media of particular social relevance' speaks to the broader tensions of books as manufactured—and in the case of many print books, mass produced—objects which are bought and sold in an often fraught economic market (Koegler and Norrick-Rühl, 2023, p. 8). This notion is not only inherently entangled within the commercial versus culture debate but also contributes to publishing and book culture's position within broader hierarchies of culture.

Debates surrounding the exceptionality and necessity of books during the height of the COVID-19 pandemic were also perceived as evidence of the hardiness of the book market within the UK. In April 2021, the PA released data that evidenced how the publishing industry in the UK was 'resilient in the face of COVID' with Stephen Lotinga, Chief Executive of the Publishers Association suggesting that 'Publishing has proven incredibly resilient throughout the significant challenges of 2020' (Joynson, 2021). However, it is worth briefly lingering on this concept of resilience and its association to the UK publishing industry for two reasons. First, the notion of resilience was not only seen as being central to the endurance of supply chains, infrastructure, and economics throughout 2020 and 2021 (all of which feed into the functioning of publishing as a business), but resilience was also presented as key to cultural survival throughout the pandemic. While the economic impact of COVID-19 and national lockdowns on the Creative Industries was often the focus of studies and commentary during the time and immediately afterwards (see, e.g., Comunian and England, 2020; UNESCO, 2021; *COVID-19 hit the creative industries particularly hard. How can they be supported in future?*, 2022'; Snowball and Gouws, 2023), some also commented on the sociocultural benefits of the Creative Industries and therefore the importance of their survival. In September 2020, the Organisation for Economic Co-operation and Development (OECD) published a report examining the cultural and creative sectors in relation to the COVID-19 pandemic. The report argued that the cultural and creative sectors were important not only for their 'economic footprint and employment' but also for their social impact (Sacco and Travkina, 2020, p. 1), particularly in terms of mental health and well-being. The OECD argued that:

> The lockdown has made evident the importance of culture for people's well-being and mental health. . . . As identified in the recent WHO report analysing results from over 3 000 studies, arts play a major role in the prevention of ill health, promotion of health, and the management and treatment of illness across the lifespan.
>
> (Sacco and Travkina, 2020, p. 25)

Similarly, in a report published based on research from an Arts Council England funded research project 'focused on the role of the arts during the COVID-19 pandemic', Bradbury et al. found that:

> In general, people during the pandemic have recognised the wellbeing benefits of arts and cultural activities. Sixty-eight percent of a UK representative sample of respondents (n = 2,002) believed the arts affected them positively and 79% thought the same of heritage activities (28). Several studies conducted during the pandemic have found associations between engagement in arts activities and mental health and wellbeing.
>
> (Bradbury et al., 2021, p. 17)

It was just such arguments that organisations like the BA leaned on to make the case that books should be considered essential items and that bookshops should therefore remain open during national lockdowns in 2020 and 2021.

The second, and related, reason as to why discussions of resilience within publishing (and the Creative Industries more broadly) are worth further discussion is because resilience—whether in terms of personal well-being and development or macroeconomic and supply-chain stability—is part of a broader neoliberal discourse that foregrounds free markets and the placement of responsibility on the individual. Newsinger reflected on this in 2012, considering the 'neoliberal state as it emerges from the 2008 [financial] crisis' within the context of the Conservative and Liberal Democrat Coalition government formed in the UK following the 2010 election and what this meant for the economics of the Creative Industries (Newsinger, 2015, p. 311). The fiscal policies of the 2010 Coalition (and subsequent Conservative majority) government favoured austerity and cuts to spending on public services and social welfare, as well as an apparent stepping back from government funding of the arts in favour of 'philanthropic and corporate investment' (HM

Government, 2010, p. 14 quoted in Newsinger, 2015, p. 306). These factors, Newsinger argues, led to:

> [A]n acceleration of the process of dismantling the social democratic welfare state and its associated discourses under the disguise of austerity; the continued strengthening of the values and practices of the market as the only legitimate mechanisms for social and cultural action. This analysis suggests that the narrative of the creative industries discourse can be accurately understood as part of a trajectory of the commodification of culture, the continuation of trends that go back to the 1980s.
>
> (2015, p. 311)

The call from bookshops and the publishing industry to classify books as 'essential' items during national lockdowns so they would be assigned the equivalent status of food and household items (like toilet paper and cleaning products) effectively aimed to make the market value of books 'legitimate mechanisms for social and cultural action' and support.[4] In this instance, books were important not only for the economic resilience of bookshops but also for the personal resilience of individuals during lockdowns. This individualistic resilience through book consumption and reading was demonstrated by the return of the British television stalwarts Richard Madeley and Judy Finnigan, who returned to the public service broadcaster Channel 4 to host five episodes of *Richard & Judy: Keep Reading and Carry On*, a live book-club style programme broadcast from the couple's own home in May 2020. The programme, which was one of a series of programmes Channel 4 commissioned under its 'Lockdown Academy' of programming, 'commissioned to help the nation through their enforced time at home' and brought Richard and Judy's tried and tested model of televised book reviews and discussion back at a time when, as Madeley put it, 'there is one great way to escape [COVID-19 lockdowns] and that's to get completely lost in a fabulous book' (Madeley, quoted in Marsden, 2023, p. 448). Everything from the title of the show, a play on the 'Keep Calm and Carry On' Second World War motivational poster that was found in one of the UK's largest independent bookshops, Barter Books, in 2000 (Jack, 2020), to the books discussed, which included *Dear NHS: 100 Stories to Say Thank You* and *The Art of Resilience: Strategies for an Unbreakable Mind and Body*, by the athlete Ross Edgley, was a reminder, literally and figuratively, of the need for stoicism and resilience during this period in time.

Newsinger and Serafini have demonstrated how resilience can be considered a key aspect of (artistic) survival and prosperity. In their analysis of the arts and culture response to the fiscal austerity of the UK Coalition government enacted after the 2008 financial crisis, Newsinger and Serafini argue:

> The deployment of resilience in cultural policy and by individual cultural practitioners can be understood as performative: it discursively constructs

> a particular conception of the problem of austerity and the appropriate individual and organisational responses. In understanding post-crisis austerity as an opportunity to reconstruct the cultural sector in a new dynamic environment of constant adaptation to change and shock, we argue that resilience does nothing to challenge or resist neoliberal capitalism; indeed, resilience (perhaps unintentionally) reinforces its logic.
>
> (Newsinger and Serafini, 2021, p. 603)

If we replace 'austerity' and 'post-crisis' with 'lockdowns' and 'coronavirus pandemic' in the above quote, we can easily apply this examination of the neoliberal logic of resilience to the publishing industry's response to the COVID-19 pandemic. The motivation behind calls for books to be classed as essential items was not only due to their status as cultural products offering a form of escape for people during the pandemic but was also due to the precarious economic foundation of publishing which sees smaller publishers and booksellers struggle to compete against conglomerates and chains (who were able to continue to sell and distribute books even during lockdowns). As a result, the argument that books were essential items exposed the publishing industry's reliance on the logic of neoliberal capitalism to sustain itself.

The Book as Cultural Product

The exceptionalism of books as a cultural product is not a new phenomenon and has been the focus of a number of recent studies. In their 2022 study *What is a Book?*, Phillips and Kovač suggest that '[t]he evidence that books have a special status in contemporary society is not hard to find', arguing that this 'special status' has been facilitated by cultural policies and economic exemptions and benefits (Koegler and Norrick-Rühl also make this case in *Are Books Still 'Different'*?) (Phillips and Kovač, 2022, p. 35). Phillips and Kovač also note that, 'Whilst other creative industries are important for human well-being and creativity too, no direct all-encompassing policies are applied in the same way to film, television, architecture, art, craft, design, software, or games', further emphasising the exceptionalism of the book (Phillips and Kovač, 2022, p. 35). But while Phillips and Kovač show recognition for the hierarchical position of books and publishing in relation to other Creative Industries, their focus remains on maintaining the status of the book and how this has been compromised by digital developments. In their conclusion, Phillips and Kovač argue that '[w]e must preach the value of whole books and long-form reading' and that to 'maintain the book's privileges, the arguments for the value of long-form reading need to be restated' (Phillips and Kovač, 2022, p. 67). Similarly, in *Bookishness: Loving Books in a Digital Age*, Pressman argues that the object or image of the book remains central to book culture, and how people express their interest and love for books, even though 'we no longer *need* books' because 'we have other means of reading, writing, communicating and archiving' (Pressman, 2020, p. 1). For Pressman, 'bookishness is about class and consumerism. It is about constructing and projecting identity through the possession and presentation of books' (Pressman, 2020, p. 12). Over the centuries, the book and its ownership, Pressman argues, have taken on a near totemic status, arguing:

> Bookishness, as such, enacts the idea of the fetish—as it was developed from eighteenth-century European colonialists through to Karl Marx. . . . Fetish is about animating the inanimate by projecting human desire onto the nonhuman. This power of the fetishized object can be religious or mystical . . . capitalistic (in Marx's critique of capitalism and the idea of commodity fetishism), or psychological. . . . Fetishism is about thingness. So when digitization threatens the physicality of books, we see a cultural response: to fetishize the book object.
>
> (Pressman, 2020, p. 63)

It is significant that Pressman here ties Marx's notion of commodity fetishism to the fetishisation of the book as an object in a capitalist market. Marx's arguments regarding the status of commodities (identified by Marx as objects for exchange or trade) provide a framework which encapsulates the tension within the book as a cultural object which is developed, produced, and disseminated through creative labour that is often mythologised or erased.

According to Marx, once objects become commodities, the labour taken to produce the object is erased, and the value of the object, which makes it a commodity, comes from the object itself, not from the labour that has led to its creation. As a result, the value of the commodity, or cultural product, can seem inherent and independent from the labour behind it (Marx, 1993). Indeed, the *work* of publishing, the creative labour from author to bookseller, and the conditions of such labour, is often removed from the equation. When it comes to book publishing in the UK (and elsewhere), the cultural product is fetishised and the creative labour producing that product mythologised, to the point that the industry is built, as this and the previous chapter has shown, on unstable foundations of fabled meritocracy, inequity, and so-called passionate work.

As previously noted, book publishing is not unique in its status as a Creative Industry that relies on troubling labour practices and expectations. Nonetheless, what may be unique to publishing is that the cultural product that comes from such labour facilitates the perpetuation of these problematic practices due to its elevated status as a symbol of culture and knowledge. Because the object of the book seemingly holds so much cultural power, it is almost irrelevant what the contents of the book are because it is the product, or commodity, itself that represents value in the market. As a result, the mythology surrounding the book as a cultural object trickles down to the processes of cultural production, leading to the erasure of the work of many of those in the industry, while at the same time the exceptional status of the book (and publishing) continues to cultivate aspiration to work in the industry despite its flaws.

Notes

1 For full disclosure, the author is a lecturer on the MSc Publishing programme at Edinburgh Napier University.
2 For more on the specific friction in bookselling and commercialism, Miller's *Reluctant Capitalists: Bookselling and the Culture of Consumption* (2006) provides an interesting historic and contemporaneous insight into the issue in the US market.
3 There were instances of supermarkets in the UK preventing customers from buying 'non-essential' items, such as clothes, kitchen appliances, books, and home furnishings, which fuelled debates regarding the value of commodities and categorisations of essential versus non-essential goods. See Garrity (2020) and P. A. Media (2020).
4 This idea of books being as essential as food is not unique to the pandemic. Writing in 1988, Marion Boyars, who was described as a 'pioneer publisher of the avant-garde', suggested that: 'The book is essential to our survival as cooked food—we need words on paper to be contemplated at leisure and annotated at will as much as we need cooked food for pleasure and nourishments' (Owen, 1988, p. 119).

References

Ali, K. (2022) 'The labour of publishing', *The Bookseller*. Available at: https://www.thebookseller.com/comment/the-labour-of-publishing (Accessed: 16 May 2023).

Banks, M. (2007) *The Politics of Cultural Work*. London: Palgrave Macmillan.

Banks, M. and Hesmondhalgh, D. (2009) 'Looking for work in creative industries policy', *International Journal of Cultural Policy*, 15(4), pp. 415–430. Available at: https://doi.org/10.1080/10286630902923323.

Baverstock, A., Bowen, S. and Carey, S. (2008) *How to Get a Job in Publishing: A Really Practical Guide to Careers in Books and Magazines*. A&C Black.

Baverstock, A., Bowen, S. and Carey, S. (2023) *How to Get a Job in Publishing: A Guide to Careers in the Booktrade, Magazines and Communications*. 2nd edn. Abingdon, Oxon; New York: Routledge.

Bennett, T. (2018) '"Essential—Passion for music": Affirming, critiquing, and practising passionate work in creative industries', In L. Martin and N. Wilson (eds.) *The Palgrave Handbook of Creativity at Work*. Cham: Springer International Publishing, pp. 431–459. Available at: https://doi.org/10.1007/978-3-319-77350-6_21.

The Bookseller. (2021) 'Enormous step forward' as BTBS affordable housing opens for applications', *The Bookseller*. Available at: https://www.

thebookseller.com/news/enormous-step-forward-btbs-affordable-housing-opens-applications-1238327 (Accessed: 28 October 2024).

Bourdieu, P. (1993) *The Field of Cultural Production*. Cambridge: Polity.

Bradbury, A. et al. (2021) *The Role of the Arts during the COVID-19 Pandemic*. London: University College London.

Brook, O., O'Brien, D. and Taylor, M. (2018) *Panic! Social Class, Taste and Inequalities in the Creative Industries*. London: Arts Emergency.

Brook, O., O'Brien, D. and Taylor, M. (2020) '"There's no way that you get paid to do the arts": Unpaid labour across the cultural and creative life course', *Sociological Research Online*, 25(4), pp. 571–588. Available at: https://doi.org/10.1177/1360780419895291.

Campbell, M. (2020) '"Shit is hard, yo": Young people making a living in the creative industries', *International Journal of Cultural Policy*, 26(4), pp. 524–543. Available at: https://doi.org/10.1080/10286632.2018.1547380.

Chandler, M. (2020) 'Innovative indies find online silver lining as coronavirus closes stores', *The Bookseller*. Available at: https://www.thebookseller.com/news/innovative-indies-find-online-silver-lining-coronavirus-closes-stores-1197721 (Accessed: 21 June 2023).

Comerford, R. (2020) 'Bloomsbury reveals plans to support indies amid pandemic', *The Bookseller*. Available at: https://www.thebookseller.com/news/bloomsbury-reveals-plans-support-indies-amid-pandemic-1199569 (Accessed: 21 June 2023).

Comunian, R. and England, L. (2020) 'Creative and cultural work without filters: COVID-19 and exposed precarity in the creative economy', *Cultural Trends*, 29(2), pp. 112–128. Available at: https://doi.org/10.1080/09548963.2020.1770577.

Conor, B., Gill, R. and Taylor, S. (2015) 'Gender and creative labour', *The Sociological Review*, 63(1_suppl), pp. 1–22. Available at: https://doi.org/10.1111/1467–954X.12237.

Cowdrey, K. (2017) 'Hachette and BTBS to tackle 'prohibitively expensive' London accommodation', *The Bookseller*. Available at: https://www.thebookseller.com/news/hachette-tackles-prohibitively-expensive-london-btbs-543206 (Accessed: 28 October 2024).

Creative Access. (2024) 'The class ceiling in the creative industries'. London: Creative Access and FleishmanHillardUK.

Creus, A., Clares-Gavilán, J. and Sánchez-Navarro, J. (2020) 'What's your game? Passion and precariousness in the digital game industry from a gameworker's perspective', *Creative Industries Journal*, 13(3), pp. 196–213. Available at: https://doi.org/10.1080/17510694.2019.1685302.

Eichhorn, K. and Milne, H. (2016) 'Labours of love and cutting remarks: The affective economies of editing', In D. Irvine and S. Kamboureli (eds.) *Editing as Cultural Practice in Canada*. Wilfrid Laurier University Press, pp. 189–198. Available at: https://doi.org/10.51644/9781771120937–014.

Find a Masters. (no date) 'How much does a masters cost in the UK in 2024? find out!', *www.FindAMasters.com*. Available at: https://www.findamasters.com/guides/masters-study-in-uk/cost (Accessed: 28 October 2024).

Flood, A. (2020a) 'Delivery by skateboard? Coronavirus sees indie booksellers get inventive', *The Guardian*, 16 March. Available at: https://www.theguardian.com/books/2020/mar/16/coronavirus-indie-booksellers-inventive-sales (Accessed: 21 June 2023).

Flood, A. (2020b) 'England's bookshops should be classed as essential, booksellers argue', *The Guardian*, 10 November. Available at: https://www.theguardian.com/books/2020/nov/10/englands-bookshops-should-be-classed-as-essential-booksellers-argue (Accessed: 20 July 2023).

Flood, A. (2020c) 'Research finds reading books has surged in lockdown', *The Guardian*, 15 May. Available at: https://www.theguardian.com/books/2020/may/15/research-reading-books-surged-lockdown-thrillers-crime (Accessed: 21 June 2023).

Garrity, A. (2020) 'Some Walmart, Target, and Costco stores are banned from selling non-essential items', *Yahoo Finance*. Available at: https://finance.yahoo.com/news/walmart-target-costco-stores-banned−173500936.html (Accessed: 20 July 2023).

Hesmondhalgh, D. (2010) 'User-generated content, free labour and the cultural industries | ephemeral journal', *Ephemera*, 10(3/4), pp. 267–284.

Houston, P. (2022) 'Cost of living crisis', *Institute for Government*. Available at: https://www.instituteforgovernment.org.uk/explainer/cost-living-crisis (Accessed: 28 October 2024).

Jack, M. (2020) 'How we made the Keep Calm and Carry On poster', *The Guardian*, 20 April. Available at: https://www.theguardian.com/artanddesign/2020/apr/20/how-we-made-keep-calm-and-carry-on-poster (Accessed: 28 October 2024).

Joynson, J. (2021) 'Publishing in 2020: Resilient in the face of COVID', *Publishers Association*, 27 April. Available at: https://www.publishers.org.uk/publishing-in-2020/ (Accessed: 20 July 2023).

Koegler, C. and Norrick-Rühl, C. (2023) *Are Books Still 'Different'?: Literature as Culture and Commodity in a Digital Age*. Cambridge: Cambridge University Press (Elements in Publishing and Book Culture).

Littler, J. (2017) *Against Meritocracy: Culture, Power and Myths of Mobility*. Taylor & Francis. Available at: https://directory.doabooks.org/handle/20.500.12854/33628 (Accessed: 26 October 2024).

Majdan, R. (2023) 'Significant cost barrier in creative industries', *Creative Access*. Available at: https://creativeaccess.org.uk/cost-of-living-significant-barrier-to-accessing-creative-industries-for-under-represented-talent/ (Accessed: 28 October 2024).

Marsden, S. (2023) 'Keep reading and carry on: Mediated reading during COVID-19', In A. Ensslin, J. Round and B. Thomas (eds) *The Routledge Companion to Literary Media*. Routledge.

Marx, K. (1993) *Capital Volume 1*. Translated by B. Fowkes. Middlesex: Penguin Books and New Left Review.

McRobbie, A. (2016) *Be Creative: Making a Living in the New Culture Industries*. Newark, United Kingdom: Polity Press.

Miller, L.J. (2006) *Reluctant Capitalists: Bookselling and the Culture of Consumption*. Chicago, IL: University of Chicago Press.

Newsinger, J. (2015) ‘A cultural shock doctrine? Austerity, the neoliberal state and the creative industries discourse’, *Media, Culture & Society*, 37(2), pp. 302–313. Available at: https://doi.org/10.1177/0163443714560134.

Newsinger, J. and Serafini, P. (2021) ‘Performative resilience: How the arts and culture support austerity in post-crisis capitalism’, *European Journal of Cultural Studies*, 24(2), pp. 589–605. Available at: https://doi.org/10.1177/1367549419886038.

Owen, P. (ed.). (1988) *Publishing—The Future: By Leading Publishers*. London: Peter Owen.

P. A. Media. (2020) ‘Supermarkets in Wales given discretion over ban on selling non-essential items’, *The Guardian*, 25 October. Available at: https://www.theguardian.com/world/2020/oct/25/supermarkets-in-wales-given-discretion-over-ban-on-selling-non-essential-items-firebreak-lockdown (Accessed: 20 July 2023).

Phillips, A. and Kovač, M. (2022) *Is This a Book?*. Cambridge University Press.

Pressman, J. (2020) *Bookishness: Loving Books in a Digital Age*. New York: Columbia Press University.

The Publishing Post. (no date). Available at: https://www.thepublishing-post.com/ (Accessed: 16 May 2023).

The Reading Agency. (2020) *New Survey Says Reading Connects a Nation in Lockdown | Reading Agency*. Available at: https://readingagency.org.uk/news/media/new-survey-says-reading-connects-a-nation-in-lockdown.html (Accessed: 21 June 2023).

Sacco, P.L. and Travkina, E. (2020) *Culture Shock: COVID-19 and the Cultural and Creative Sectors*. OECD.

Shade, L.R. and Jacobson, J. (2015) ‘Hungry for the Job: Gender, unpaid internships, and the creative industries’, *The Sociological Review*, 63(1_suppl), pp. 188–205. Available at: https://doi.org/10.1111/1467–954X.12249.

Siebert, S. and Wilson, F. (2013) ‘All work and no pay: consequences of unpaid work in the creative industries’, *Work, Employment and Society*, 27(4), pp. 711–721. Available at: https://doi.org/10.1177/0950017012474708.

Snowball, J.D. and Gouws, A. (2023) ‘The impact of COVID-19 on the cultural and creative industries: Determinants of vulnerability and estimated recovery times’, *Cultural Trends* [Preprint]. Available at: https://www.tandfonline.com/doi/abs/10.1080/09548963.2022.2073198 (Accessed: 17 December 2024).

Squires, C. (2017) ‘Taste and/or big data?: Post-digital editorial selection’, *Critical Quarterly*, 59(3), pp. 24–38. Available at: https://doi.org/10.1111/criq.12361.

Squires, C. (2020a) ‘Essential? Different? Exceptional? The book trade and COVID-19’, *C21 Literature: Journal of 21st-Century Writing*, 10 December. Available at: https://c21.openlibhums.org/news/403/ (Accessed: 20 July 2023).

Squires, C. (2020b) *Sensing the Novel/Seeing the Book/Selling the Goods*. In: Lazendorfer T & Norrick-Ruhl C (eds.) The Novel as Network: Forms, Ideas, Commodities. New Directions in Book History. Basingstoke: Palgrave Macmillan, pp. 251–270. Available at: http://dspace.stir.ac.uk/handle/1893/31484 (Accessed: 27 October 2024).

Stevenson, I. (2019) 'Distribution and Bookselling'. In Andrew Nash, Claire Squires and I. R. Willison, eds,. *The Cambridge History of the Book in Britain Volume 7: The Twentieth Century and Beyond.* Cambridge: Cambridge University Press, pp. 191–230.

SYP. (no date) 'Welcome to the society of Young publishers', *The Society of Young Publishers*. Available at: https://thesyp.org.uk/ (Accessed: 16 May 2023).

Turner, M. (1988) 'The Publishing Group: The End of Publishing as we know it?', in Publishing: The Future: By Leading Publishers, ed. by Peter Owen. Peter Owen: London, pp. 12–21.

UNESCO, (2021) *Cultural and Creative Industries In the Face of COVID-19: An Economic Impact Outlook.*

Wood, Z. (2023) 'Indie bookshop numbers hit 10-year high in 2022 defying brutal UK retail year', *The Guardian*, 6 January. Available at: https://www.theguardian.com/books/2023/jan/06/indie-bookshop-numbers-hit-10-year-high-in-2022-defying-brutal-uk-retail-year (Accessed: 21 June 2023).

Conclusion

In his collection of essays deliberating on the business of books, *So Many Books*, Gabriel Zaid argues that 'Book people', which he identifies as authors, readers, publishers, booksellers, librarians, and teachers, 'have a habit of feeling sorry for themselves' despite there being little need for this as '[t]he book business, unlike newspapers, films, and television, is viable on a small scale', meaning that every book does not need to sell millions of copies in order to be financially viable (Zaid, 2004, p. 26). While Zaid's comment is technically correct—it is possible for a publisher (or author, given the increase in, and ease of, self-publishing) to approach book publishing on a small, even artisanal, scale and perhaps break even (if not be entirely profitable)—in reality, book publishing is a multi-billion pound industry focused on the mass production of a ubiquitous cultural product that permeates almost all aspects of life. From board books for babies, to specialist manuals for professionals and businesses, books are a cultural product that sit at the intersection of where the object as utilitarian artefact *and* cultural signifier meets. This is not a novel observation. The status of the book as a cultural product has been analysed for decades. However, what is often missing from these conversations, at least in relation to book publishing in the UK, is a discussion about how the book industry sits alongside other Creative Industries, such as film and television, crafts, video games, and museums and galleries, in terms of cultural policy and how culture(s) and heritage are characterised. Indeed, publishing has not received the same kind of examination of its position as a Creative Industry in relation to neoliberal ideals of free-market capitalism, despite being one of the most economically dominant sectors of the creative industries.

To return to Zaid's comment that book people can 'feel sorry' for themselves, it is true that not all stakeholders in the industry see this fiscal success. We know that consumer publishing is much more financially volatile than academic or educational publishing, and given that this is the part of the industry that is 'front facing', in terms of encompassing the more mainstream aspects of book publishing that most reader-consumers engage with, it is perhaps understandable that book publishing has acquired a reputation of being precarious (and therefore risk-averse) and unpredictable. However,

DOI: 10.4324/9781003187905-5

rather than focus on the precarity of the status of the cultural product itself, which is well-trodden ground, this book, taking the lead from similar studies into other Creative Industries in the UK, has considered this uncertainty in terms of the people and practices behind the book. What it reveals is how, despite maintaining a particularly romantic and mythologised reputation as an industry in which the superior status of the book as a cultural object persists, there are significant systemic issues regarding the configuration of the industry in terms of its workforce and, as a result, what is published. As discussed in Chapter 2, publishing is one of the worst Creative Industries in terms of representation of people from working-class backgrounds working in the sector. Moreover, while the representation in terms of race and ethnicity may appear to match national averages of workforce representation, the fact that London remains the hub of the publishing industry (as it is for other Creative Industries) and has a much higher proportion of individuals from ethnic minority backgrounds than the rest of the country undermines the impression that publishing is a more equitable Creative Industry in terms of race and ethnicity.

As Chapter 3 demonstrated, the cultural cachet and talismanic status of the book as a cultural object have enabled the industry to maintain its aura of exclusivity. The self-mythologising of the creative work of publishing, which many in and adjacent to the industry perpetuate and promote despite also recognising the exploitative practices of publishing that can rely on an individual's passion and love for the work, sustains its reputation as being a particularly coveted Creative Industry to work in. This is not unique to publishing, as many Creative Industries are stuck in this cycle of offering attractive, even glamourous, creative work that is precarious and exclusive, but the purpose of this study was to bring such issues to the fore in order to provide a basis by which publishing as a Creative Industry can be understood and interrogated.

One aspect of this book which was unexpected was how much the COVID-19 pandemic and subsequent national and international lockdowns would feature. However, it is impossible to discuss contemporary publishing and book culture (and culture more broadly) without considering the impact of the global coronavirus pandemic, given that it provided a backdrop by which to examine how the cultural and commercial elements of publishing are measured. Calls for books to be classed as 'essential' items not only revealed how the book was considered to be important to the country's health and well-being but also, perhaps inadvertently, emphasised the economic imperatives of the industry. The national lockdowns in 2020 and 2021 shut down many of the venues and spaces which facilitated engagement with the cultural outputs of other Creative Industries—museums, galleries, cinemas, and concert venues all had to close—but books, items that can be enjoyed alone, in the safety of one's own home, were viewed by the book trade as a unique cultural product that could provide escape where other forms of culture could not. This once again empowered those in the industry to stress that books are 'different'.

But are books, and the industry behind them, really different? This contextualisation of the publishing industry in the UK within the broader discussions of the Creative Industries also provides an opportunity to scrutinise the industry via frameworks of existing Cultural Studies scholarship. Such scholarship, as this book demonstrates, often provides points of comparison or expansion that can advance understandings of book publishing in the UK, and there are many areas of enquiry this small volume was unable to investigate, which warrant further investigation. Such as, for example, how the publishing industry directly intersects with other Creative Industries (e.g. in the licencing and adaptation of books to film and television) and how such relationships operate in terms of the creative labour involved. Or critical evaluations of whether publishing industry interventions which aim to improve equitable representation in workforce demographics are having the intended impact. Indeed, it is hoped that this book might act as a starting off point for these, and other, areas of exploration.

In practice of this crossing of scholarly insights into publishing (as a Creative Industry), this book will end on an optimistic note instigated by the work of Banks' *Creative Justice*. As Banks notes, alluding to the multitude of empirical studies and industry reports that have evidenced inequities in creative work, 'it's no longer sufficient to say that working lives in the cultural industries are unknown to us' and that it is 'well known that the allegedly universal benefits of the creative economy are proving elusive for the majority and tending mainly to accrue to the privileged few' (Banks, 2017, p. 4). However, while acknowledging that such work remains important, Banks also calls for a focus on creative justice to both the cultural product and cultural work itself. For Banks, this means moving away from the focus on the economic value of the cultural product and reaffirming 'a sense of the objective qualities of culture and the aesthetic', in addition to viewing 'cultural work as a source of (not just) an economic value, but also a social value, as well as an aesthetic one, underwritten by different kinds of political sensibilities' (Banks, 2017, p. 2). Banks acknowledges that neither of these propositions are intended to be 'reactionary' or call for an uncritical romanticisation of creative artefacts and creative work, and it would be counterproductive to promote such a reading of Banks' work at the end of a study which has criticised these very issues within publishing. However, Banks' call for creative justice, particularly in terms of creative work, encourages 'the "internal" goods and qualities of work as a practice—but without discounting the "external" structures and pressures that tend to make such work somewhat less than appealing, and often deeply unfair and unjust' (Banks, 2017, p. 2). Accordingly, this book ends on a cautiously optimistic note that as examinations of publishing as a Creative

Industry develop, they do so within this context of creative justice and respect for both the cultural product *and* the cultural worker.

References

Banks, M. (2017) *Creative Justice: Cultural Industries, Work and Inequality*. London: Rowman & Littlefield International, Ltd.

Zaid, G. (2004) *So Many Books*. London: Sort of Books.

Index

For Product Safety Concerns and Information please contact our EU representative GPSR@taylorandfrancis.com
Taylor & Francis Verlag GmbH, Kaufingerstraße 24, 80331 München, Germany

www.ingramcontent.com/pod-product-compliance
Lightning Source LLC
LaVergne TN
LVHW010937110826
845149LV00013B/2643

* 9 7 8 1 0 3 2 0 3 5 5 2 9 *